Sarah Akwisombe is the South London 'no bullshit' influencer and entrepreneur who transformed her life using her understanding of money-manifesting techniques. Instead of going job to job with no savings, or much to show for her work life, she now has a thriving six-figure business. Sarah reached success when she launched her online education business, the No Bull Business School, and started documenting her journey to financial success.

sarahakwisombe.com

THE MONEY IS COMING

YOUR GUIDE TO MANIFESTING MORE MONEY

Sarah Akwisombe

PIATKUS

PIATKUS

First published in Great Britain in 2020 by Piatkus

1 3 5 7 9 10 8 6 4 2

A CIP catalogue record for this book
is available from the British Library.

ISBN 978-0-349-42577-1

Typeset in Lato by M Rules
Printed and bound in Great Britain by
Clays Ltd, Elcograf S.p.A.

Papers used by Piatkus are from well-managed forests
and other responsible sources.

Piatkus
An imprint of
Little, Brown Book Group
Carmelite House
50 Victoria Embankment
London EC4Y 0DZ

An Hachette UK Company
www.hachette.co.uk

www.littlebrown.co.uk

To Marley, who was my cheerleader the whole way through writing, and bubba Mia. Right now, you are both too little for this book to be useful to you, but as you grow up, I hope it helps you on your journey to becoming the incredible women I know you'll be.

Love,
Mummy x

CONTENTS

FOREWORD

by Jen MacFarlane, aka The Money Medium

What you will realise very shortly is that mastering money has a lot more to do with mastering deeper parts of *yourself* than the actual money.

I'm sure you've watched and read many things on manifesting, as it has gone pretty mainstream in the last few years. But one thing that I find is missing in a lot of these dreamy, elusive approaches to manifesting is that nobody is teaching the deeper elements of self-mastery that are needed to transform and change the way you are with money.

I'm so proud of what Sarah has been able to bring into *The Money is Coming*. She is a true leader and a wise soul. This book is just what the world needs at this time. It truly is time in our human evolution to mix that dreamy/visionary side of manifesting with deeper levels of self-development and practicality.

Sarah and I have worked together for several years now,

and what an amazing transformation it has been. This is my favourite part of working with people: watching them transform into a clearer, bad-ass, amazing version of themselves.

I remember the first session we had. Although she was initially a bit reluctant to 'spill the beans', Sarah had the drive to really change her programmed blocks. She knew there were deeper things holding her back from bigger things. Let's say that again:

THERE WERE DEEPER THINGS HOLDING HER BACK FROM BIGGER THINGS.

Oh man, this girl's mind was filled with big dreams!

We worked through many of these deeper things: relationships, negative money thoughts, the conversations around money that she had been involved in, being too humble, not admitting what she really wanted, fears and having to push herself to order the lobster instead of the cheapest item on the menu.

Let me tell you, this woman moved her ass! She pushed herself out of her comfort zone and did the work. Trust me, at first that work can feel like you're busting through an old skin and getting used to a new one every day. It isn't exactly comfortable. It's actually uncomfortable as heck, but the outcome is transformative. It can literally change your life, as it did Sarah's.

Within a year Sarah was messaging me, sharing six-figure numbers. She was giving to and supporting charities and projects that were aligned with her heart and there was this glow about her – like she really knew now that anything was possible. The possibilities really were limitless. She had integrated the tools into her life and knew how to step into action to make impossible things possible. It was like watching a tree grow branches that fully bloom and burst into beautiful, aromatic orange blossoms.

When working together, it has always been a mission for Sarah and me to be a part of balancing the financial system on this planet, and that can't happen unless we all take responsibility for our part in growing our own abundance. More money in the hands of more people with good hearts, compassion and empathy will truly transform this world.

This is a book that will transform and change your life, how you think and the actions you take. If I were you, I'd get ready to say yes to opportunities that are coming your way. If you're ready to attract more money, you'd better get ready to receive it, because, honey, The Money is Coming!

You are capable of absolutely anything.

Richest blessings,
Jen

INTRODUCTION

Money. It's a big, loaded, heavy subject. It plays a massive part in society, in our idea of success and in how we value ourselves as people. It can do damage and be the cause of greed and sadness, but on the flip side, if used correctly, it has the power to transform lives for the better.

You've picked up this book because you want to change your situation, and I'm going to help you do that. But it might not go down in the way that you're expecting.

Here's what I mean.

Money is affected by our mindset, more so than most people realise. I believe that there is some quite magical, spiritual stuff that goes down when it comes to money – if, that is, you stay positive. You may have heard this referred to as the Law of Attraction or manifesting.

Manifesting is the idea of being able to think about something and hold it in your mind, then have it appear or be 'attracted' to you in real life. In this book, we are going to be focusing on you becoming able to manifest more money into your life.

The Law of Attraction is the belief that if you think positively, you will attract positive things into your life – and the same goes for negative thinking attracting negative things. You can see how manifesting and the Law of Attraction go hand in hand, as they are both about using your mindset to create real-life outcomes.

Throughout the book, I'll be covering the psychological and spiritual sides of your money mindset, and sharing some easy practices and exercises that you can use day to day to create a more positive money mindset, opening you up to receiving more money.

As much as I love the idea of things just magically happening for us, at the end of the day, my brain is rooted in logic, and I'm sure the same is true for most of you reading this. I can't always make sense of something 'magic' unless it has a psychological, reasonable element that makes sense to me. I'm also a straight-talking girl from south London who needs the realness – no bullshit.

On the other hand, I am obsessed with spirituality, astrology, crystals – you name it. I've seen these things seep into mainstream culture over the past couple of years, and I often make business decisions based on something that happens in a tarot card reading or how I feel about it intuitively, rather than just following what makes sense on paper. I truly believe that in the future more people will tune into this 'magic', and it will become quite normal. As the world around us seems to go to shit, I think we will begin to look to something bigger than us for guidance and a sense of hope.

So, as you can imagine, when I sat down to write a book on money mindset that would incorporate both the practical and metaphysical, I knew it was going to be challenging. I am, after all, a mass of contradictions. On the one hand, I need to see evidence to believe something, but on the other hand, occasionally something will happen that is completely unexplainable in the traditional sense, leaving me lost for words. I can't explain *why* it has happened, but I can identify a feeling of universal intervention. This can make me question everything I know.

But do you know what I realised? We are multifaceted humans. Not everything is black and white, and we have no idea of everything we know and don't know. It's important to be open-minded and realise that, sometimes, it is completely normal and OK to have two opposing thoughts or beliefs at exactly the same time.

In this book, I want to make the ideas of money and manifesting make sense, open your mind to new avenues of thinking and encourage you to question everything. I'm not writing this to people covered in purple crushed velvet, pulling tarot cards and burning incense (although I'm not gonna lie, I'm totally into that now – Palo Santo for the win); I'm writing to real folk.

This is for the person on the 7.49 train from East Croydon to London Victoria on their way to the office job they hate. Because I've been there. And I know you need this. I know that, as fun as the magical stuff is, it also needs to make *sense*.

I've read a lot of books on manifesting and the Law of Attraction in my time. I felt they all missed a certain crucial element: the 'Yeah, but how does it actually *work*?' vibe.

I'd read one of those books and I'd get excited for a moment. I'd believe for a minute. I'd feel like I could make more money and I'd be on a high for a few days. But it would all fade away as soon as I had one setback. And when you're deep in the pits of money problems – bills coming out of your arsehole, debt mounting, wanting stuff you can't afford, feeling like you'll never get on top of it all and struggling to buy the special 'ripe and ready' avocados at Waitrose (#first-worldproblems) – those setbacks come often.

It's taken me a while to find something that sticks, and more importantly, to understand why it has stuck.

My grandmother was a counsellor and my mother is one too. As much as I resisted it for many years of my life, I believe that what happens in our formative years can have a huge impact on who we become as adults. While I by no means have the patience to be a counsellor myself (sitting and listening to people talk without being able to jump in with my own opinion would be torture for me), I do have huge respect for the work that they and psychotherapists do. So, you'll find a good smattering of psychological the-ories in this book. I'm not going to pretend I know every theory inside and out, but I will do my best to explain what I take them to mean in layman's terms and why I believe they are relevant to your money journey.

I am also a big science geek. I like to know and understand

the science behind how things work, because something about science seems ... correct. Factual. So, where I can find scientific theories or studies that prove a point, I'll share them. I'll make it no bullshit. Because ain't nobody got time to get a PhD in order to make a little more cash.

Magic-feeling things *have* happened to me since I started on my own 'money journey'. Things that didn't make any logical sense, no matter how hard I tried to find some. I constantly go back and forth between the facts of a situation and the magical or spiritual side of it, and I don't think I'm alone in that.

As you read through this book, you will understand it is less about prescribing exactly how you should do things, but instead about urging you to explore the area of money on a deeper level. Some elements are scientific, some are spiritual.

Lastly, I'm not religious, but I will make references to religions – and I will use the word 'universe' a lot. Please don't chuck out this book based on that! I want you to take that word as whatever it means to you. To some it may be a god; to some it might be your gut instinct; to some it may be your consciousness or your mindset; to some it might be a spirit guide or a fairy that lives in the woods under a toadstool. Whatever works for you, babe! 'Universe' is simply the word I like to use because it feels all-encompassing. I believe that there is something out there bigger than us, but I don't feel a need to define exactly what that is. So when you see me use the word 'universe', that's open to your interpretation.

Since embarking on my money and manifesting journey, my entire belief system and financial situation has shifted. This is what I want to happen for you. Because you wouldn't have picked this book up if you had a shit-ton in the bank, would you?

Here are a few cool things that I've managed to manifest since I started doing this manifesting stuff.

- I went from making barely £18k a year and struggling to pay bills to creating my own business with a six-figure turnover (and taking home a nice chunk of that as my own salary).
- My husband was able to quit his job.
- We bought our dream house after being told, year after year, that it couldn't happen.
- I've had things miraculously show up, like designer clothing, trips abroad and bespoke kitchens. I'm not going to lie, some of it is down to my job as an influencer. But trust me, some of this stuff was way too coincidental to put down to only that, and you'll hear some of these stories throughout the book.
- I've gone from feeling anxious at restaurants with friends, ordering the cheapest thing on the menu and only drinking water, afraid that my card was going to get declined, to now picking whatever I want on the menu – I'm talking lobster *and* steak – and not even looking at the bill.

These changes might sound privileged, even frivolous. I know I haven't had it bad. Some people are in completely incomparable situations and are starting out many steps behind. I really hope that this book can provide hope and guidance to you, no matter what your current situation.

Without generalising, we have all, at some time, experienced anxiety and stress about money. No matter what you have in the bank, if your money mindset isn't positive, you will still be stressing. That's how big an issue money is in our society. I've heard from people who have much more money than I do, yet are still grappling with money mindset issues.

A positive money mindset is less about what you have in the bank and more about how you think. Here are the most important, long-term mindset changes that happened for me once I started working on my money mindset.

I no longer believe that money makes you evil. I believe money is a tool and can be energised with whatever intention you give it. Bad person: bad intention. Good person: good intention. Money in itself does not cause this.

I no longer believe that people with money are greedy. Some of the most charitable, philanthropical and generous people I have met come from wealth. I have seen the amazing things money can do for the world and society, and I'm here for it.

I no longer believe that money is a man's game. I've seen that women are just as capable, if not *more* capable, at making this money stuff work for them. They're more inclined to believe. And you know what? I've seen how important it is that the power so often wrapped up in money – usually money held by men – is more evenly distributed. I believe more women should have money in order to play bigger roles in the decisions that currently get made for us. I feel incredibly passionately about this and it's why I try and spread the word as much as I can about this stuff. It's not just so that us girls can go and buy pretty handbags (though I ain't mad at that for one second), it's because the way the world runs is based on cash flow: and, damn it girl, we need more of it! We women should be on equal footing with our partners, making more financial decisions for our own futures and those of our children. Period.

Most important? **I rarely ever feel stressed about money anymore.** Honestly. It's like a HUGE weight has been lifted off my shoulders and now I can enjoy life for all of the reasons that exist beyond basic survival. It's taken me three years to get to where I am now. And, boy oh boy, I'm still just at the beginning.

This is big stuff, but it's simple. And you can learn it within a few weeks.

Before we get down to business, I should tell you how

this started for me. How I met the lady who changed all my beliefs and helped me to expand my learning and go from barely making minimum wage to creating a six-figure business.

MY MONEY MANIFESTING JOURNEY

At the age of twenty-eight, I had a one-year-old baby and a full-time job as a content editor for an online business platform. That job had turned me into the 'breadwinner' of the family. My husband, who worked in legal admin for an insurance company, had cut his working hours down to three days a week so that he could look after our daughter, a far cheaper solution than us both working full-time and paying for childcare.

All was seemingly going well: I was earning £40k a year, the highest salary I'd ever been paid in my life. We had a little bit of leftover money each month, enough to start some savings for our daughter and afford to treat ourselves to a nice dinner here and there. We had our own flat that we were paying the mortgage on, and we could slowly redecorate and renovate it to our own tastes – I'd always had a passion for interior design. We rolled like that for about a year and a half, and things seemed to be looking up from the days of scrabbling to pay bills and having direct debit payments bounce left, right and centre. Our debt was clearing slowly. Aside from my work environment being rather toxic, I actually enjoyed the work I was doing, and I felt accomplished at it. Times were good.

Then one day, out of the blue, I got fired. I had a strange feeling when, on the first day of annual leave I'd booked, I received an urgent text telling me I needed to meet my boss in person, in an hour.

'Why on earth would I just *need* to meet him in person, on the first day of my week off?' I asked my husband. I think we both knew the answer.

As I walked into the meeting, I knew what was coming. There had been friction between me and the CEO of the company, and on top of that I suspected that the company was struggling financially, as I'd been paid late quite a few times. I should tell you something about me now: I'm fucking self-righteous. I'm not easy to manage, and I now know that I make a terrible employee. I was on one of the highest salaries there, and I didn't take any shit. When 5 p.m. rolled around each day, I was out of that office like there was a fire under my ass. If an email was sent at 5 p.m. that required me to stay in the office for another few hours, I'd simply pretend I hadn't seen it and go home. They weren't paying me overtime, so why should I stay? I had a baby daughter at home who needed her mummy. (Plus I wanted to get the hell out of that toxic environment and get home to work on the fun interior design blog that I'd started on the side; but I digress.) As I said, I had a feeling it was coming.

At the meeting, I was handed an envelope and told I'd

been 'let go'. A clause in my contract meant that they only needed to give me a month's notice (and, seemingly, no warning). They blamed finances and said that they were removing my position from the company.

I walked home in a daze. I was seriously panicked. While I tried to look on the bright side, to see the positives and find meaning in why I had been fired, I cannot lie. I was shitting my pants. We were now down to less than £13k between us for the year – unless I pulled some money in, and FAST.

While working at this office job, I had been building up my interior design blog on the side. I really enjoyed it, and I could see myself having a career in interior design. From my past entrepreneurial endeavours (once as a recording artist and once as a make-up agency owner) I'd learned that, if you can build a brand and community online, you have a great shot at launching your own freelance career or business. The day I got fired (after the initial shit-yourself moment), I took it as a sign from the universe and I decided to go full-time with my blog. I'd been working with a few brands along the way and I'd picked up some paid freelance work, so I figured that the time was now or never to go all in on what I loved.

After a few months, we were doing OK. And by 'OK', I mean we were just about surviving. Bills were still being missed. We struggled to make ends meet each month. There sure as hell wasn't any leftover money, and our daughter's savings fund was put on indefinite hold. I was approaching thirty, and things were not as I had thought they would be for such a significant milestone. I felt like an absolute failure.

When I was much younger and had envisioned turning thirty, I'd imagined I'd own multiple properties, have a successful business, a family, more money than I knew what to do with and be able take holidays whenever I felt like it. I imagined this powerhouse female, carrying Chanel bags and talking loudly and assertively into a phone while someone made me coffee. I'm not quite sure why these were my markers of what success looked like, but we will come to that later.

I'd watched *The Secret*. I had a made myself a vision book, which was like a multi-page mood board of all the things I wanted to achieve in life. In it, I had created vision boards for myself, sticking motivational images of high-flying women and the things I wanted to own and experience. Cars, furniture, property, holidays, fashion – it was all there. On the first page of that book I had written a note to myself: 'This book is dedicated to the pursuit of becoming a millionaire by my thirtieth birthday.'

Looking back on this notion I had of where I would be when turning thirty, I laugh, as it sits at such odds with what I was saying and believing every day when it came to money after losing my £40k salary. It's as if I was in denial about how unhappy I was being broke, so it became something I justified. I would openly talk about how I'd never be rich and how I thought people with money were show-offs. 'Who would spend two grand on a bag?!' I'd say judgementally, laughing with my friends over dinner. Yet that was the very image of success that I had long held for myself. What a bloody paradox.

Knowing what I know now, there was not a chance in hell that I was ever going to become a millionaire at thirty. Not because it isn't possible to do so, but because I was living and speaking in complete opposition to what I wanted. I was out of alignment, and even my own thoughts and actions were in conflict.

It took us about a year to really get back on our feet.

At most, I was making minimum wage with my freelance work and blog collaborations. On the bright side, it was enough for me to justify doing it full-time. I was freelancing and I was making ends meet. This, as I quickly learned, was something that a lot of the women who followed me on social media wanted to achieve, too. I'd built up a small but engaged online following via my blog, and soon I was getting questions about what my 'secret sauce' was.

'How did you do it?' they'd ask.

'I didn't have a choice!' I'd say.

Getting fired means you just have to get on with it. But I soon realised that I was obviously doing something right. Perhaps my previous experience of building a music career and working in tech start-ups had given me an inside advantage. I started to pick apart everything I'd learned and began compiling it into a kind of dossier.

One day, I realised that I could perhaps package this

material up into a course that I could teach online. In (yet another) previous job, I'd taught kids about music production, so I knew that I could teach fairly well. I spent some time putting together an outline for a course that would cover every single thing I'd ever learned about building a blog and making a living from it. Not, like, hundreds of thousands of pounds, by any means: but enough to live on, which seemed to be what these women wanted. They just wanted to be able to earn a living doing something they loved. A simple request, yet one that has, for years, seemed unrealistic. But now it's possible.

Once I had the outline for the course, I set up a PayPal link for £69 (which was way too cheap for the time and effort I was putting in, but we will discuss this later in the book – see Chapter 8) and I put it out to my social media followers and the readers of my blog. I launched it at around 8 p.m., switched off the laptop, watched some TV and later went to bed.

I woke up the next morning to dozens of PayPal notifications. Overnight, I had made almost £5k.

£5k, guys!

FIVE GRAND.

This was the most money I'd ever made by myself, from scratch, EVER. I was in total shock.

By the time I closed enrolment a few days later, I had totalled almost £13k of sales. For a course I hadn't even properly written yet.

I was completely and utterly blown away.

This was the first major shift in how I thought about money. At this point, I realised three things.

1. It could actually be quite easy to make money.
2. I COULD make money doing something I loved.
3. I bloody enjoyed this feeling! I wanted more! Fuck being broke! Why had I pretended I was happy with it?

I felt like my whole world had changed. I felt like I had been shown the light.

In that moment, I suddenly realised that I had been figuratively shitting on myself. I had done it out of sadness, out of a desperation not to feel 'less than', out of wanting to fit in with my peers who were all also struggling financially, out of denial, out of bitterness, out of depression. And by doing so, I was holding myself back from ever being financially free. Holding myself back from allowing money to come into my life and being able to enjoy it.

I made a vow then and there, approaching thirty and having made, on my own, my first 'big' amount of money, that things were going to change. I wasn't going to shit on myself any longer.

Where would I find someone who could help me work all this out? There were business coaches, sure. But this was different: it was purely a *money mindset* thing. Where could I go?

I went where any smart person goes: the internet. I

headed to one of the many Facebook business groups in which I had, until then, just been a silent observer, and wrote my first post. These people don't know me, I thought. So I just let it all out.

'I'm sick of being broke. I know there is more out there for me and my family. I don't want to pretend I enjoy or am OK with this mediocre life anymore. I want the money to be everything I've always dreamed of being, and to be able to give my family everything I've always dreamed of giving them. I know that I am the problem. How I think is the problem. Is there anyone out there who might know of someone who could help coach me through this? Not, like, a financial coach but more a money manifestation-type coach?'

It felt so cathartic. It was the first time I had ever said (or typed) to anyone that I was feeling this way. It was the first time I had admitted it, even to myself.

Within seconds, the thread was popping off. Tens of coaches suddenly appeared, each wanting to be my best friend. 'I can help you with this!', 'I am soooooo successful!', yada yada. It was overwhelming, and I was turned off. I sensed a bunch of money-grabbing sharks who saw me as a piece of fresh meat, ready for the taking. They all sounded the same. I was disheartened. Everything about their reactions had reinforced what I thought I knew: as soon as you talked about money, everyone wanted a piece for themselves.

A few hours later, my Facebook inbox pinged. The message was from a lady called Jen MacFarlane. She went by the name 'The Money Medium'.

Hi Sarah! This is my speciality! I just released a book called Think Create Jump. It's about overcoming the limitations of the mind – first, you have to know your own programming! Then we go to work with reprogramming techniques! I'd love to set up a free Skype call with you if you would like to seriously bust through the blocks. :)

Hold up.

A *free* Skype call? Hell yeah! No one else had offered anything like that. No one else had taken the time to message me privately. I might as well try it, I thought. Nothing to lose. And did I mention it was free?!

Within days I had my first call with Jen. We couldn't have been more different in some ways. We lived thousands of miles away from each other, me in busy London, surrounded by skyscrapers, Jen in Banff, Canada, surrounded by snow-capped mountains. Jen talked about crystals and energies and vibes and the universe. I spoke about logic and how things needed to make sense for me to believe in them.

Yet, despite these differences, we just ... clicked.

Jen swore a lot, like me. She got that I couldn't dive fully into crystals and chanting instantly, and she respected that. She was easy to chat to. She didn't take herself too seriously (and I needed that!). She was warm and kind, and I felt I could trust her. She got me to open up about things that I'd never spoken to anyone about, at least not in any kind of depth. I felt like I could be honest with her, instead of having to put on a sarcastic, dismissive breeziness.

I had a feeling that working with Jen, combined with reading and absorbing all of the information I could find out there on money and manifesting, could change my life.

In time, it did. I want to reveal how I did it, and show you that you can do it, too.

Jen and I have since gone on to become close friends. We have even created an online Money and Manifesting course together, which has been one of our biggest successes to date.

LET'S GET STARTED ON YOUR MANIFESTING JOURNEY!

In this book, I'll be sharing my ten-step method to change how you think about money and how you attract money – forever.

I can almost guarantee that, if you follow each step, you will automatically start to feel more excited about your financial future. You'll have a richer, more fulfilling life, even if the actual amount of money in your bank account stays the same.

But I don't think it will!

I'm not going to tell you it will be easy; it won't. Especially if you've grown up in a working-class environment. It's likely your friends and family will think you're a nut job or try to give you a 'reality check' here or there. They mean well.

There may be some casualties along the way. But if you're serious – and I mean REALLY SERIOUS – about changing your financial future, you'll need to be willing to stand on your own and really go through some uncomfortable, yet cathartic, processes.

Because before you make money, you have to become **the kind of person** who can make money.

You ready? Buckle up. It's gonna be a ride.

CHAPTER 1

YOU'VE BEEN PROGRAMMED – AND YOU DIDN'T EVEN KNOW

From the day we are born, we start absorbing the world around us: sights, smells, colours, sounds. We learn what danger is and what hurts us, and we also quickly learn who is on our side. We learn who will protect us from harm, shoulder any burdens and shield us from destructive influence.

We've all heard of social conditioning, right? According to Wikipedia, it's:

... the sociological process of training individuals in a society to respond in a manner generally approved by the society in general and peer groups within society. The concept is stronger than that of socialisation, which is the process of inheriting norms, customs and ideologies.[1]

In English? We inherit shit – ideas that people perceive to be 'normal'. We inherit them from our parents and our grandparents, from the society and culture that have come before us. We are also influenced by stuff all around us without realising, for example, the things our friends say, or what's being shown in the news. If you think back to how your parents behaved around money when you were a kid, that's likely to have a whole lot of influence on the way you think about money now.

We need to break down our negative money blocks and tackle this social conditioning, or programming, so that we can begin to change our financial situation. Think of this conditioning as the foundation of everything you believe you 'know' about money. Because let me tell you, what you *believe* you know ain't actually what is happening in the world!

We each have our own internal 'map of the world', so to speak. But for each person, that map will be different. That's why a liberal left-winger will have a hard time understanding a right-wing, middle-aged, Trumponian view. Their internal maps of the world are just SO different that it can often be a struggle to see eye to eye.

You need to get to know your map of the world and how you have been programmed in order to change your mindset. As we are addressing your money mindset, you need to understand the financial elements of your programming.

Some examples of negative money programming might be:

'I can only make X amount a year in this job, tops.'

'Money is the root of all evil.'

'People with money are douchebags.'

'Money controls my life.'

A negative money belief is anything that is currently stopping you from feeling good about money, making more money or enjoying the money you already have. Some common themes are guilt, judgement, shame and blame.

We typically inherit these beliefs from our parents, our friends or, of course, society and the media. We tend to develop a belief system that isn't always our own. Which, when you think about it, takes the piss!

Most people don't even know about their money programming until they have analysed it. I mean, how often does someone ask you about your beliefs around money? Or how you feel about money? How everyone felt about money in your household growing up? When does anyone talk about money openly . . . ever?! When I started working with Jen, these are the types of questions she would throw at me via our Skype sessions. They made me squirm and wriggle. I hated them. They were alien and made me feel pretty damn vulnerable.

There are four key areas that invade our brains and affect how we think about money.

PARENTS

Growing up, your parents or carers mean everything to you and, as a child, you constantly seek their approval. The thing is, not all parents have life figured out. I mean, no one does! So, it would be weird to assume that, once you reproduce and have kids, you suddenly attain the perfect neutral base to raise a child without inflicting any of your own damaged views or opinions on them.

How does this relate to money, and more specifically, your money?

Because you've been programmed to inherit and be influenced by opinions and views from all around you. As a child, what your parents thought about money and how they talked about it would have had a massive effect on you. And I do mean HUGE. In our formative years we take on those opinions and views as gospel. As we grow up, we tend to mimic this behaviour to get a positive response from our parents. We don't even realise we are doing it; it becomes internalised.

Psychologist Carl Rogers explains:

A condition of worth arises when the positive regard of a significant other is conditional, when the individual feels that in some respects he is prized and in others not. Gradually this same attitude is assimilated into his own self-regard complex, and he values an experience positively or negatively solely because of these conditions of worth which he has taken over from others, not because the experience enhances or fails to enhance his organism.[2]

In layman's terms, conditions of worth are the messages about what we need to do in order to be valued by people. These conditions are built up from when we receive positive praise or recognition. They are shaped by your family and society, and if you go on to have kids, you'll likely pass them on to your own children. If I, as a kid, keep getting loads of praise and positive regard heaped on me every time I eat my broccoli, I'm damn sure more likely to grow up as someone who believes that it's good to eat healthily. That may even become one of my own conditions of worth – to eat well.

Let's swap broccoli for money. Let's imagine you grew up with parents who had strong conditions of worth around charity. Take a minute to think about where they created their own conditions of worth. You guessed it ... THEIR PARENTS. It's like a big old funnel of conditions of worth just being passed down through the generations, over and over again.

Let's say your parents' beliefs were that you shouldn't use money for your own personal gain: that if you have leftover money, you should give it to charity. You may have heard this spoken about as a youngster; maybe your mum and dad were having a quiet chat over dinner about their friends who had just splashed out on a new car when they 'could have helped someone with that money'.

At this young age, those thoughts aren't your own. But you hear them, over and over again. You recognise that your dad doesn't seem happy when he talks about his friends who were 'selfish' with their money. You think he seems angry. Because you recognise the emotions that go along with it, you take that on board as something *not* to do.

As an adult, it's likely that this would then show up in the form of guilt. You want to buy something nice for yourself, but you hear a little voice in your head saying, 'That's a waste of money. You could be helping someone in need with that money instead of being selfish.'

Sound familiar?

Money programming from our parents comes in myriad forms. For example, you could have been exposed to frivolous spending, in which case you might have a problem with saving as an adult. Or you may have had parents who were always sensible with their money and never took on debt, in which case, as an adult, you may find it hard to be in debt or to borrow money from people as it makes you feel like less of a person.

You take on others' conditions of worth as your own. Often, their views become your views. Even if they're not your actual views, they will for sure become a little whispering voice on your shoulder, making you feel like shit about every financial decision you make.

So that's the biggie. Our parents (or whoever you grew up around: a carer, a grandparent, anyone you looked up to or was an authority figure) have programmed you, unknowingly, to have certain thoughts and feelings around money. These thoughts and feelings could be positive! But a lot of the time they're not.

Carl Rogers also talked about developing your own 'locus of internal evaluation'. Simply put, this is when you create your own judgements around whether something is good or bad. You decide internally, rather than externally.

Here's an example of internal evaluation.

I just went for a run. I feel really good about it! This time last year I couldn't even jog down the street let alone around the whole block without stopping. I get such a rush afterwards and I feel so proud of myself. I can see my skin is glowing more and my fitness levels have come up. I really can't believe it; I feel so good.

Here is an example of external evaluation.

I just went for a run. I've been trying really hard and my boyfriend says I'm doing well. When I get back from a run, I like to tell him what I've done. Hearing him say he is proud of me makes me feel really good. I haven't had anyone say they can see that I've lost weight, though, and I've been working so hard. It makes me wonder if it's all worth it.

Can you see how the external evaluation can be problematic? You are relying on outsiders to make you feel good rather than finding that inside yourself. Carl Rogers's belief is that you will be much happier if you can find your own internal evaluation; after all, you can't always control how others will react.

With that in mind, here comes your first exercise. There are no right or wrong answers, at this point we are just trying to build up an understanding of how we think about money, as it's not something you'd naturally observe every day.

> ## ♟ *EXERCISE* ♟
>
> **Journal about what you heard about money growing up.**
> - What was your parents' attitude to money?
> - What did they say about it?
> - Do you remember any particular phrases being used, such as 'Money doesn't grow on trees,' and the like?
>
> **Now journal about what you saw of money growing up.**
> - Was it abundant in your house?
> - Did you buy nice things?
> - Were you always scraping for the next meal?
>
> **What do you think are your inherited beliefs around money?**
> Take a moment to write down the first three things that come to mind.

So, we've examined where our original conditions of worth around money have come from. And you'd think it would be as simple as that, right? I mean, that's a bloody revelation in itself!

Oh no, my friend; there's plenty more where that came from.

THE MEDIA

Cast your mind back to every movie you've ever watched that has a particular focus on money: *The Wolf of Wall Street*, *Boiler Room*, *The Social Network*, *The Big Short*, any heist movie, or any movie with a wealthy father figure. Nothing good ever comes of it, right? The moral of the story is always 'money can't buy you happiness', or, if we're going to be blunt about it, 'money makes you a greedy douchebag who forgets to pick up their kid from school'.

Here are some examples. See how many you can recognise from your favourite movies.

The greedy person

Person gets rich fast, usually to the detriment of someone else. They get greedy, take loads of drugs, then fuck up their life (e.g. *The Wolf of Wall Street*, *Scarface*).

The bad parent

Person values money over family, is always working really hard and putting business meetings ahead of their kids. They have a 'realisation' moment, usually through being trapped somewhere with their children, that family is the most important thing. They shun their career forever (e.g. *Family Man*).

The too-busy businesswoman

Woman on top: she's a busy businesswoman who values her career over her relationship. Her husband feels emasculated by her wealth and significance and cheats on her with a younger woman. She realises she has placed too much value on her work and takes off on a journey to 'find herself' (e.g. *Eat, Pray, Love*).

The loon

This character has all the money yet is quiet and mysterious. Almost scary in their approach, they may be a psychopath – or maybe just sad and depressed because, after all, money can't buy you happiness (e.g. *The Great Gatsby, Marie Antoinette, American Psycho*).

The con artist

They seem wealthy, but where did all that money come from? Did they murder someone? Is it all counterfeit? (E.g. *The Talented Mr Ripley, Catch Me if You Can*.)

The broken-hearted

A rich girl is being married off to another rich man by her pushy parents, who only care about being part of the elite. She falls in love with a poor yet lovable underdog and, realising that she would rather have love than money, runs away with him. (e.g. *Cruel Intentions, Romeo and Juliet, Clueless*).

Time and time again we are shown these stereotypes – and these are just the first few that came to mind! In these movies, the protagonist only seems to become more human once they shun the world of money and instead remember their 'real values' of family and friendship and 'being a good person'. There is ALWAYS a moral lesson, because, it seems, Hollywood likes to hate on money. Funny, coming from one of the most glamorous and money-laced industries in the world.

Now, I'm not saying that family, friends and being a good person aren't real values. But I don't believe that holding these values and having or wanting money are mutually exclusive. I've only worked this out recently. It's a story we see played out in the media often. It's generic as hell, but for some reason people lap it up.

I only realised how much what we see in the media affects us when it crept into my personal life. I went through a period of being the 'breadwinner' in my relationship. Because of everything I'd seen in the media throughout my life, I believed I was the 'too-busy businesswoman' stereotype. I actually had no evidence to support this – my husband was pretty happy, and he definitely hadn't cheated on me – but because this stereotype was the only representation I could find of a woman like me in the media, I got it into my head that he was being emasculated.

Surely he couldn't deal with me earning more than him? Surely me running the business made him feel small? I would push and push and push these ideas on to my husband, no matter how many times he told me that he wasn't feeling any of those things at all.

One day I twigged what was going on.

I'd never seen a representation of a woman who had made more money than her husband where it had all been OK. Instead, I had seen lots of examples of cheating and relationship breakdowns.

Now, I'm sure there are some positive money movies, TV shows and news stories out there, but you can't deny that it's these negative ones that capture our attention the most. It seems humans just *loooove* predictability. That constant exposure really does get inside your brain, at least until you're aware of it. Then you can start to catch it, like the early bird to the worm.

Here's a challenge for you. In the space below, write the

name of one movie that you've seen that offers a positive angle on money.

Not that easy to think of one, is it?!

FRIENDS

Ah, friends. Love 'em, hate 'em. They can build you up and cut you down within seconds.

That old adage of 'you are the average of the five people you spend the most time with' seems particularly apt when applied to money. Because you don't only inherit your money beliefs from your parents; your friends have a big part to play in that, too.

I've found that friends rarely talk about money in a positive light. If money is being discussed, it's usually something to bitch and moan about – or perhaps you are indulging in a quick round of my old favourite game, 'Who is the most skint this week?'

Jade is £60 over her overdraft!

Michael just had his mortgage payment bounce!

Hayley just had her card declined!

Claire just had to miss out on a holiday because she couldn't afford the airfare and now everyone is going without her!

OMG, guys! Let's all just sit in a circle and jerk each other off over how broke we all are!

MAKE. IT. STOP.

For some reason, when people get together and the topic of money comes up, the tone seems to turn negative. It's so rare to hear someone talk positively about how much they've made or want to make. It's seen as showing off or bragging.

No one wants to be the first person to approach a positive money conversation, because they're likely to be shot down with responses like, 'Well, hoping to make a hundred grand in a year isn't that realistic, Susan.' Friends love to come up with what they think is helpful 'real talk', but is often actually a projection of their own fears and desires.

We keep ourselves all neatly tucked in and say what everyone else says and react to things in the same way that everyone else reacts. We don't want to stand out or have everyone start gossiping about us behind our backs. It's just easier to fit in.

Here's your friend challenge: at your next dinner or drinks, see if money gets brought up. Observe. Is there a positive or negative discussion? If positive, great! If negative, try to keep your own comments strictly positive. We will delve deeper into your money vocabulary later.

CULTURE

Oh, you thought we were done with inherited beliefs? Nope. Because, believe it or not, the geographical area of the world you live in can also have a knock-on effect on how you think about money. I'm British. Here in the UK, I have noticed that the cultural tendency is to treat talking about money, along with any displays of wealth, as being particularly uncouth. This seems odd to me. In a country that has literally been built from wealth, we seem to feel the need to keep it all hidden away from public display for fear of judgement. What's with that?!

As the years go on, this is changing, but talk to most older generations of British people and it's seen as quite crass to talk about or be excited by money. I'm absolutely pooing my pants about the fact that my grandparents might be reading this right now, because I can almost guarantee they won't agree with it. And if someone, somewhere up your lineage is thinking those thoughts, then they've probably been passed down the line to you. Remember what you've just learned about conditions of worth!

When I went to LA recently, I was happily surprised by how people in the States are willing to pay for convenience. It's big business. Valet parking at restaurants, drive-through everything ... spending your money in this way is treated as a right. It's not considered to be frivolous or lazy: it's just part of the culture. On the contrary, in the UK, this kind of thing would be seen as indulgent and unnecessary, much to my annoyance! I'm here for that convenience! Americans also seem to be all about that self-made life. It seems to me that you can get into any circles in the US as long as you have money. They don't seem to mind where it came from. You have some money? Cool, you're part of the club. In the UK, no matter how much money you have, how you acquired it is very important. Won the lottery? You're still not going to be part of the elite. Born into wealth? Well, welcome to the middle class. The class system still rides strong here, and it influences people's idea of worthiness.

I remember being absolutely blown away going to my first Nigerian wedding. I watched as people used dollar bills to 'spray' (throw money at) the bride and groom. I'd never seen such an outward display of wealth, but portrayed in such a fun and loving way. It had nothing but good vibes attached to it and I thoroughly enjoyed it. What a way to start your marriage, hey: having money thrown at you by your loved ones! It felt really uplifting.

These cultural tendencies can infiltrate our thinking – and that makes sense, right? If you live somewhere where the overall thought patterns are similar, or most of society thinks in a certain way, it's only natural to play along, almost without realising. You may find yourself judging or looking down on how people interact with money.

BREAKING DOWN YOUR PROGRAMMING

For now, let's summarise everything you've learned so far about your money programming.

We know that four major factors influence our own thought patterns around money: our parents, the media, our friends and culture. We also now understand that, through no fault of our own, we have developed conditions of worth that have been cultivated by society.

How do we start to break down any programming that we have unknowingly picked up? I like to use a method that is rooted in CBT (Cognitive Behavioural Therapy). It's something my mum taught me, and it works really well when it comes to examining where you've picked up all these bizarre thoughts about money, and working out how to break them down, so that you can start to reach the 'true you' underneath. This 'true you', as I like to call it, is what psychologists refer to as 'the organismic self'. It's basically child-you, the un-messed-with version of you, one who can think for herself and make her own decisions about shit. It's the true, authentic you. Not the one we present to the world, not the one with all the messed-up social condition-ing. Just pure, unadulterated YOU. Most people don't even know what this looks like, because their 'true you' is buried beneath so many layers of OPB (Other People's Bullshit).

Unfortunately for us, these conditions of worth meant that, as we grew up, we actually learned to prioritise the positive regard we get from other people over our own thoughts and feelings about ourselves. Remember the inner and external locus of evaluation? How messed up is that?

Over the course of this book, I will aim to help you strip down those layers of OPB and get back to the real you: how *you* feel about money, how you *want* to feel about money, and how to live with that unashamedly.

As I said, it won't be easy, but it's possible. Because if I did it, so can you.

⚑ *EXERCISE* ⚑

Let's end this chapter with a little bit of homework. You can download a handy PDF worksheet for this at www.themoneyiscoming.com

1. Look at the beliefs you wrote down earlier that you have inherited about money. An example might be 'I believe that money is hard to make'.

2. Ask yourself where that belief comes from. Did your parents display that to you in their behaviour or words when you were growing up?

3. How does this belief have a knock-on effect in your day-to-day life? For example, believing that it is hard to make money may stop you from trying out new things, as you might see them as pointless or too much effort.

4. Dispute these beliefs with evidence. Imagine that you are in court and you are on the stand pleading your belief's case. The opposing lawyer comes at you with evidence to dispute what you're saying. For example, 'You say money is hard to make, but there was that one time when you got paid five hundred pounds for that quick job that was really easy.' Write at least one piece of disputing evidence alongside your negative money beliefs.

You can repeat these four steps with all of negative beliefs you have around money. I should also say that, if you have inherited some positive money beliefs, GREAT! We don't want to start messing with those!

What's important to remember is that you are not stripping away layers of yourself. You are stripping away layers of conditioning in order to discover your true self and be more open and excited about money.

$

CHAPTER 2

YOU'RE COCK-BLOCKING YOURSELF

I didn't think I'd be beginning this chapter with a Bible quote. I definitely didn't think I'd be beginning this chapter with a Bible quote that I saw on Khloe Kardashian's Instagram stories, but here we are. The universe has ways of surprising and delighting me daily.

This quote is from Matthew 7:2.

> For with whatever judgment you judge, you
>   will be judged;
> and with whatever measure you measure, it
>   will be measured to you.

Let's look at how this fits into the context of manifesting money. Because trust me, my man Matthew had this shit down.

In my first proper session with my manifesting coach, Jen, she jumped straight in and asked me what my beliefs were about money. I found it a strange question: one I hadn't ever thought about before and had never been asked by anyone I knew. I wasn't really sure how to answer.

'Umm ... I'm not sure. It's stressful. It causes me stress.'

'Go on,' she said.

'It disappears easily,' I said. 'I don't get to use it in the way I want. It's got a bad vibe. It's trying to punish me.'

'How does it feel when you look in your wallet and see money?'

'It has a bad vibe. Like it's working against me. And it's never there anyway!'

Jen smiled as I talked. But not in a way that suggested she was welcoming my words. She was smiling at me in a way that was ... cheeky. Like a teacher asking a child a question and then sitting back and enjoying watching their brain put the pieces together.

'OK,' she said. 'And how about people who have money: how do you feel about them?'

This required much less effort to think about. 'People who have money are show-offs,' I said. 'Vain. Greedy. Selfish. Out for themselves. Buying themselves designer handbags and driving fancy cars, just to get attention. They're always talking about money and all the great stuff they have ... I'm not like that.'

The silence after those words came out of my mouth felt very loud. I'd never said anything like that before.

Wow.

It sounded pretty harsh. I didn't like myself saying those words.

It seemed I did have some strong beliefs about money after all. And it hadn't taken much to pull them to the surface as soon as I was asked. As I spoke, I felt a tightening in my stomach. I felt tense. Dark, almost. It didn't feel like the light, easy-breezy way I think and talk about money now.

I felt a bit disgusted with myself, actually. I was . . . bitter.

'Do you think that money is going to be attracted to you when you feel like it has a bad vibe and that it's your enemy?' Jen asked.

Shit. Lightbulb moment.

'Probably not,' I said. Of course it bloody wouldn't!

After all, I'd read *The Secret*. I'd listened to podcasts on the Law of Attraction. The number one rule is 'like attracts like'. So, me thinking that money had a bad vibe while still hoping to attract it just didn't make any sense to, like, the universe. But I hadn't thought that this was the problem. I thought the problem was . . .

Well, actually, I didn't know what the problem was.

I didn't know why I didn't have more money in my life, because I was working my ass off. It just all seemed to slip through my fingers and go on paying bills or unexpected expenses before I had a chance to enjoy it. It was spent just surviving.

My attitude had been that the problem was definitely not

me. It was someone – or something – else's fault. The whole system was rigged, and someone like me would never be able to work it to my advantage.

'Do you think there are people out there with money who do good in the world?' asked Jen.

'Um, maybe,' I said. They seemed few and far between.

But I knew, logically, that yes, of course there were. My mind went to Bill Gates. Since 2013, he has donated more than £28 billion to various charities and social causes, championing health and education. I say I knew that *logically*. But I couldn't *feel* it. It seemed like Bill Gates was an anomaly. And, after all, people like him can afford to do such things – they're mega billionaires! Contributions like that should be required of billionaires. They owe it to us: the people. The ninety-nine per cent.

I remember ending that session with Jen feeling a bit flat. I'd just spent a figure I really couldn't afford at the time, hoping to learn about how to manifest more money – and all that had happened was I'd been presented with a few questions, had someone smirk at me, and then been left to it. What had I done? I could have used that money to pay a bill, but instead I'd skipped paying it in order to cover the session. What an idiot.

Where were all these magical tips that would make me a millionaire, make cash turn up, help opportunities arise?

Maybe this wasn't worth it after all.

I closed my laptop and went to go and hang out with my husband Jason in the living room.

'How was the session, babe?' he asked.

'Yeah, all right,' I answered in a dull tone. 'She just asked me loads of weird questions about how I felt about people with money and stuff.'

'And?' he said.

'And I told her what I think. People with money are douchebags. Who needs to spend two grand on a Chanel bag? Like, what kind of pointlessness is that? When you could spend it on something that matters, like putting it towards a deposit for a house, or paying off a credit card, or something.'

Jason laughed. 'You sound like your dad talking about flying first class.'

We both vividly remembered that conversation, even though it had been years ago. It had been hilarious. My dad is the type who is very clear in expressing his opinions, thanks to a private school education and a degree in politics (or economics, or something like that). It's usually quite funny and keeps us all entertained, plus it gives us some material for doing impressions of him later. I think he hams up his rants sometimes, because he knows we find it amusing.

We had been talking about what it would be like to fly first class. I can't remember how the conversation had come up, nor why he felt so passionately about it, but I remember him saying, 'Why on earth would you spend an extra five thousand pounds just to fly in a separate part of the plane and eat with a metal knife and fork?! It's ridiculous!'

I thought back to that moment and realised I was modelling my dad's behaviour. His opinions. His thoughts. Spending two thousand pounds on a Chanel bag is probably *not* something my dad would think that highly of. He would probably consider people who did so idiots. I realised, in that moment, that this was why I also thought they were, indeed, idiots.

Remember those conditions of worth we learned about in Chapter 1? I had become the person that all children grow up wanting to be: someone who makes their parents proud of them. And I'd done that by starting to have the same opinions and sharing them, loudly, whenever anyone would listen.

Now, let me tell you, I didn't work all of this out at the time. This is stuff that I've since explored and developed, mostly since being asked to write this book. But in that moment, talking to Jason about how the session with Jen had gone, I had a major awakening: I'd taken on a lot of my father's opinions about people with money, even the ones that might have really just been him messing around and overexaggerating because he knew we were finding his ranting amusing.

I had a belief about money that was in direct contradiction to where I wanted to go. After all, I was seeing a coach to help me manifest more money, but at the same time, I thought people who had money were idiots and show-offs who were only concerned with themselves. Even in these early stages, just a few hours after my first call with Jen, I could see I wasn't making any sense. My thoughts were in complete opposition to what I was trying to achieve.

I was cock-blocking myself.

I judged how people spent money. Therefore, I consciously worried about people judging how *I* would spend money (when I actually, finally got some) – because, of course, they would think the same way as me, right?!

If you remember that whole 'map of the world' thing, you'll know that no, they wouldn't. But at the time, I believed my map was the only map.

This belief had had an invisible hold over me for my entire life. It had stopped me from talking about wanting to make money, for fear of coming across as greedy. It had stopped me from being positive about money in any way whatsoever, for fear of being judged. It had stopped me from chasing goals or had led me to see certain goals as 'unrealistic'. It had kept me in exactly the same financial position for years.

> For with whatever judgment you judge, you
>   will be judged;
> and with whatever measure you measure, it
>   will be measured to you.

Had the universe simply been giving me more of what I said and believed?

I started to think about how the things I thought, and the things I said out loud around my friends, would sound to the universe: the big man, the Law of Attraction, karma, magic – or whatever it was.

I talked about how broke I was. Often.

I relished sitting with friends and moaning about being skint. Often.

I judged and openly criticised people who had money. Often.

I daydreamed about the day I would have money and all the things I'd do with it, but then I'd find secret joy in cussing out people who had money, being incredibly judgemental about how they spent it. At the end of the day, I was jealous and bitter.

But, straight up, I had no fucking excuse for such judgemental behaviour. I'd come from a fairly wealthy family who had provided me with many privileges growing up. I was being an ungrateful cow.

I knew that, in truth, not everyone who had money was a bad person. I only had to look at my grandfather, who had gifted me part of the deposit to buy my first flat, to know that. He had the money to do it. He was wealthy and wanted to use his wealth to help others, both within his family and outside it. I knew *he* wasn't a bad person.

I also knew, if I was honest with myself, that buying a Chanel bag doesn't make you a bad person, either. Maybe the person buying the bag just likes it. Maybe it'll retain value and become an heirloom piece for their children. Maybe they had worked their ass off and always dreamed of buying this one thing to celebrate their work. Maybe they just walked past, wanted it, could afford it, and so bought it.

And why shouldn't they?

Why was any of this my concern? Why is it your concern?

Because we are jealous, bitter and judgemental.

I imagine money is the number one thing that causes resentment, jealousy and bitterness among humans. We see it play out on a major scale every day. Think back to how many times you have heard people talk about how wealthy people should solve the world's problems, or simply 'give it all away'.

Here's something to ponder.

Within days of the 2019 fire at Notre-Dame, at least €500 million was raised for the reconstruction of the landmark. I've heard countless opinions on this and seen many memes and social media posts saying things like, 'The rich should be doing more for the world! Why is Notre-Dame getting all this funding while around the world we are still recovering from tragedies that actually killed people?'

The first thing I want to say is that the media have a direct interest in keeping us 'normals' hating the wealthiest two per cent. Why? Because it's likely that ninety-eight per cent of people will feel bitterness, jealousy or resentment towards that two per cent: they have it easy, right?! Now, I'm not saying the wealth distribution doesn't need to be better; but the fact is, getting people riled up about what the rich are doing sells papers.

Back to Notre-Dame.

You're cock-blocking yourself

I understand the sadness and resentment that people must feel when they see that a tragedy with no human victims has led to a huge amount of money being donated in just a few days, when there are people who are suffering more serious consequences around the globe due to various social, economic and health issues. I get that. I think anyone would. Because on paper, it doesn't make sense. It doesn't make sense that actual humans should suffer when, in the same world, an old building is rescued so quickly.

Except that, when you pull your head out of your own opinion, your own map of the world, it makes total sense.

Why?

The people who donated money to the restoration of Notre-Dame felt very strongly about supporting the project. It was of personal significance to them. And ultimately, people can do whatever they want with their own money.

I'll say it again, louder for the people in the back!

People are allowed to do whatever they want with their own money.

It's theirs, they own it, they decide. The same way you decide what to do with yours. Just because someone is rich doesn't mean they are obligated to do anything. Whether you think they should or shouldn't do something is of no significance. You have your opinion and your idea of what's 'right', but theirs might be different. Your beliefs come from your own internal map of the world. You live different lives, with different values and different perspectives.

Sure, it's a nice idea for the rich to help the poorer or more needy in society. And yes, personally, as soon as I started making money, I found ways to give back. It's of importance to me. But I do it on my terms, in the way that I want to. I give what I want to give, and I give what I feel personally comfortable with in this moment. I will not be shamed or pushed into doing anything just because someone else thinks that it's the right thing to do. Just because you believe that something is right or valid doesn't mean you should shame people into doing it.

Imagine yourself in the future, having worked your little butt off to become financially stable, wealthy, or perhaps even rich. Just imagine it for a second. You have plans about how you are going to use that money for causes that you support, ideas that you want to see come to fruition, or perhaps to provide stability and security for your future descendants. You've planned these things for years, since before you had any of this. Then, all of a sudden, someone comes along who hasn't ever walked a mile in your shoes and tells you how to spend your money. They start to spread messages about you in the media. They start to tell everyone you're greedy. They shout abuse at you in the street. They say you're selfish, and you don't care about anyone else but yourself. But they don't know what you do behind closed doors.

I think you'd be pretty damn cheesed off.

So why do we do it to others if we wouldn't like it ourselves?

This judgement is so normalised that we don't even realise it's happening. It's just a friend at a dinner party joking about the woman who bought a new handbag, our dad complaining about flying first class, someone sharing a meme or a post on Facebook about how selfish rich people are.

These kinds of micro-judgements about how money is spent or used directly contradict attracting money. They also contradict who you need to become in order to start making serious money moves.

It might take a while for this to sink in, and it might feel completely wrong. It feels wrong because we are currently in that ninety-eight per cent who are groomed daily to hate the rich and blame them for the world's problems.

It feels wrong because you're still judging.

You're still talking out loud about how you hate money.

You're still judging how other people spend theirs, even though it shouldn't be of any concern to you because everyone has their own life and is entitled to do whatever they want with their own money, regardless of how you personally feel about it.

Let me tell you, this constant contradiction of what you want (money) versus what you say and how you act (that you hate money or dislike people who have it) is not going to serve you. You have two internal tracks running, and they conflict with each other. This messaging confuses the universe.

Here's an example of how:

Imagine that you and your partner want to get your living room decorated. You hire an interior designer, and she comes to give you a quote for the work and get an idea of what you both want. You invite her into your home, and you all sit down over a cup of tea in your current living room as you and your partner take turns in describing to her your dream living room ideas.

You go first. You want a room full of colour and patterns. You quite like having lots of little pieces around the room because they have meaning to you and they make the space feel cosy and lived in. You're obsessed with the colour green. You stayed at a hotel that had a room decorated like this once and you really liked it. It made you feel good – relaxed – and it felt aspirational to you. You get excited talking to her about it: you can almost imagine how the room will look! You can imagine how you'd feel hanging out in that room every day. You can feel the pride you'd have when guests come over. It seems so good that perhaps it couldn't even be possible. Could your dream living room really happen?! Could the designer deliver exactly what you have in your mind? Could this new room help you become the person you've always imagined you could be?

It's now your partner's turn to talk about what he wants. Except that he's not sharing what he wants: he's creating a long list of what he DOESN'T want. He doesn't want colour. He likes green, but he prefers a minimal, neutral space, because he doesn't like things to be garish. People might think it's a bit 'show-offy'. He definitely doesn't want any little bits around the room because they 'could get broken' or 'will show dust'. You listen to him talk to the designer and think to yourself, 'God, he sounds so boring. And negative!'

Your excitement diminishes as you realise you have completely different views to your partner and you're unlikely to get anything either of you is happy with.

The interior designer scratches her head with a puzzled expression. 'OK, guys. I'll see what I can do.'

Can you see what I'm getting at?

Both people are you. Let's say the first person, you, is your subconscious mind, the things you truly want. The partner is your conscious mind, the things you say out loud. The designer is the universe.

If you look at the situation through the eyes of the designer, you can see that she's confused. Perhaps she's even a little bit annoyed at having wasted her time coming over to your house when she has a long list of other clients who have been far more succinct about what they want.

This constant confusion between what you actually want versus what you say out loud causes serious problems. Faced with this, the designer would have done one of two things.

1. She might deliver something average that doesn't really surprise or delight you in any way. It's not what you envisioned, but it's OK. It'll

do. It's not provocative and it doesn't cause any awkwardness to anyone. It's middle of the road. It fits in. Your friends will say it's 'nice'. You've spent your hard-earned money on a bloody average result. So, you get put off doing it ever again and dissuade your friends from hiring an interior designer because 'it's not worth it'. You all sit around at dinner and discuss what a waste of money it was. You decide you should have never trusted someone to get it right when you 'could have done it yourself and saved the money'.

2. The designer might not call you back. She decides not to take on your work because you're too bloody difficult. You're so difficult, in fact, that she can't even try and make a start on your project. Every move she makes seems to lead to a dead end, as one of you might love it but the other one will hate it. She sits for a while trying to work it out, then gives up. She can see that this constant tug of war between you and your partner is going to cause her too much stress and the job isn't worth it. At the end of the day, you wouldn't even be grateful for a middle-of-the-road design, because it's not right for either of you. So, she decides, what's the point? When you don't hear back from her, you think about decorating the room yourself, but you never get around to it. You

end up with nothing. The room stays in its current state and frustrates you every day. When your friends come over you apologise for the state of it and say you're going to redecorate – one day. That day never comes.

You cannot begin to move forward in becoming financially free if your mind is playing tricks on you and thinking different thoughts at the same time.

When trying to attract money, two opposing thoughts created by the same mind cancel each other out. You are not sending out any signals to the universe to attract anything, because you have created a 'zero' thought. Zilch. Nada.

You will stay in the position you are in now until you start to align your conscious and subconscious thoughts. The first way you can do this is by changing your language to be more positive and open-minded. If you find yourself being judgemental about how people spend their money, stop. Change the subject. If you hear other people talking about the rich, how they spend their money, or what they 'should' be doing, don't get involved in the conversation. Even if you're not quite 'there' with the notion of becoming completely judgement-free about money or how it's spent, just don't engage.

Emancipating yourself from judgement is incredibly difficult, don't get me wrong. I'm still working on it myself. I'm not saying this task will be easy, but it has to happen in order to create the signals needed to attract money into your life. It has bonus effects too. You can apply this divorce from judgement across the board, with highly positive and calming results.

Judging someone in a bikini on Instagram? Move your thoughts on. Judging how someone is parenting their kids? Keep it moving. Judging someone's choice of partner? Get over it. It's not your concern.

Your concern is your future and becoming the person you want to be. Your concern is you living your best life, and that sure as hell isn't going to happen while you sit around wasting time judging other people. That's just bad vibes, man.

$ *EXERCISE* $

Take some time to observe any contradictory or negative thoughts and language you have about money or how other people spend it.

On one side of a piece of paper, write 'want', and on the other, write 'judgement'. Draw a line down the middle of the page. At the end of the week, make a list pairing up all the contradictory thoughts. For example, the 'want' side might say, 'I want to own a Chanel handbag,' while the 'judgement' side might say, 'How can people splurge that much money on a designer bag? What a waste.'

Start to observe where contradictory thoughts and

behaviour exist between what you actually want and how you show up and behave each day. The key step here is to become aware of these contradictions. Once you're aware of them, they won't be able to slip by, cock-blocking you on your manifesting journey.

You can download the PDF to accompany this exercise at www.themoneyiscoming.com

C

CHAPTER 3

YOU KNOW YOU WANT IT

In Roald Dahl's 1964 novel *Charlie and the Chocolate Factory*, we were introduced to a young girl by the name of Veruca Salt. Described as 'the little brute' by the Oompa-Loompas, Veruca was an only child, spoilt by her wealthy parents, and she wasn't used to hearing the word 'no'.

Veruca knew what she wanted, and she wanted it NOW.

As she made demand after demand, her poor father was left quivering in her shadow, scared to do anything but give in.

Veruca Salt has a lot to answer for in the modern world of our money mindset.

For an entire generation, we didn't associate 'I want' with assertiveness, strength or decisiveness. No, we associated it with Veruca Salt. It made us think of childish, bratty demands, made without consideration of how those demands affected anyone else. And as kids, we're constantly warned against behaving in this way.

'I want never gets.'

'Say please!'

'Don't make demands!'

We're trained to be meek and grateful for anything we do get, even if it's not what we truly wanted. Any kind of 'wanting' and you're stepping straight into Veruca Salt territory, running the risk of being forever labelled a 'bad egg'.

I realised this character had created a lot of psychological noise around how I saw other people – and myself. And I'm not the only one. This worry about coming over as 'bratty' has led to a mass epidemic of people not being honest about what they want for fear of how they will be perceived.

Over time, not being able to speak truthfully about what we want means we start to suppress our feelings. And we all know that, if we suppress them for long enough, those feelings get buried so deeply that we don't even notice them anymore. They become a deep, subconscious desire. Desires like this can become strangely at odds with the person you are in your day-to-day life.

You bury your intuitive wants and desires so deeply that you don't even know what they are any more. If some-one were to ask, the day-to-day you would answer with something completely different to what you really want, deep down.

In the previous chapter, we saw that your outward judgements are not in alignment with where you want to be. The same is true of your suppressed wants and desires.

Consciously you don't recognise these wants and desires. You definitely wouldn't use the phrase 'I want.'

I want.

Sounds abrasive, doesn't it? It conjures up images of someone perceived as bratty and spoilt. Veruca Salt.

But let's just flip that on its head for a second.

ASSERTIVENESS EQUALS SUCCESS

Assertive behaviour is behaviour which enables a person to act in his own best interests, to stand up for himself without undue anxiety, to express his honest feelings comfortably, or to exercise his own rights without denying the rights of others.[3]

When it comes to business, politics and world crises, we need people in positions of power who can be decisive. We need people who know what they want and who aren't afraid to say it. We admire this kind of assertiveness. We call it 'strong leadership'.

I find we naturally follow and look up to those who have both their subconscious and conscious wants in alignment. They're naturally persuasive and ambitious. We call them 'go-getters'. Wouldn't you like to be called a 'go-getter'?

I know I have been called one since getting my wants in alignment and speaking them out loud.

It goes without saying that we would expect someone like Winston Churchill to be able to quite clearly say what he wants, without hesitation. Or Barack Obama. Or Mark Zuckerberg. Or Robert De Niro. Or Prince.

We don't look at these types of people and think they are bratty: we think of them as doing what needs to be done, as pushing themselves and those around them to achieve the very best outcome.

It is interesting, though, that when we think about assertive women, such as Beyoncé, Madonna, Michelle Obama, Donatella Versace or Cardi B, something different happens. We might finding the word 'diva' coming up in our heads.

The idea of a 'diva' is a social construct. It's not a reality: it's just how society has labelled certain women, women that are 'go-getters'. I believe it's reductive, a way to belittle women's ambitions and drive. A woman speaking up to say how she would like something done or asking for what she wants is no different to a man doing the same. Yet when a woman does it, it can often be perceived differently.

Why is that?

Is it because women have been shushed for so long that hearing us speak openly and with strength is somehow worrying? Is it because we have spent so long *not* speaking up that to hear the odd one of us doing it now is uncomfortable?

This leads to a bigger question: do women struggle to be assertive?

We've been kept quiet for so long that, relative to men, we have work to do when it comes to using our voices to speak up for what we want.

Thankfully, we are seeing more and more women speaking up and being clear on their goals, outcomes and desires. Unashamedly so! It's refreshing and it sets a much-needed precedent for more women to talk about what they want, especially when it comes to money. But a lack of assertiveness can affect anyone, regardless of gender, and it's important that everyone works on it. Failing to do so can result in a loss of confidence, a lack of control and no steering of the ship.

Remember: being assertive = success.

'I want' is assertiveness in its most acute form. We should be excited by 'I want'! We should be delighted when we hear people use it. After all, it's clear and concise.

'I want' has definition. It cannot be misread or misunderstood. It's clear, it's to the point, it's accurate. It allows no room for error.

Why do we idolise leaders who can be assertive and say what they want, yet never let ourselves do the same?

Because saying 'I want' allows no room for other people's insecurities.

Because saying 'I want' forces you to take centre stage.

Let's unpack those a bit.

It allows no room for other people's insecurities

Saying 'I want' is bold. It makes us put ourselves first, for once. It's a proud declaration of not giving a shit about what else is going on. It's saying: 'I want this, and it's important to me; so important, that I am using the naughty words "I want".'

Some people can interpret you saying 'I want' as somehow having a direct effect on them. Somehow, when you say, 'I want', they hear it as you *taking* something, something that gets removed from them because you've taken it. Logically, we know that's not the case. This is a clear example of a 'lack mindset' in operation.

LACK MINDSET VERSUS ABUNDANCE MINDSET

A lack mindset is a mindset where everything comes from a place of missing out: not enough to go around, competitiveness, comparison. Judgement.

This lack mindset is what most of society has, and the media love to play into it. Most of us start with a lack mindset as a default position, because it's very normal. It's low-vibe. It's when you think 'realistically', or in a limited way, about what can be achieved. It can be very hard to think outside of a lack mentality, because it often causes our thoughts and fears to spiral. Panic sets in.

By contrast, an abundance mindset is one of believing that there is plenty to go around. More than enough for everyone to have their fair share. It's a high-vibe feeling, where you believe that there can be a solution to every problem. Some people also describe it as a 'growth mindset'.

A lack mindset means we pick up on problems easily and use them as a reason to not push ourselves further. An abundance mindset means we see every problem as a challenge that has a solution, one which just needs to be discovered. That is the mindset I want you to have by the time you finish this book, because it is exactly what is going to help you start attracting more money into your life.

Someone else saying what they want shouldn't have a negative impact on you. It's what they want, and they are proudly declaring it. Great! Good for them! What does that have to do with you?

All it does is hold up a mirror to your own inability to say what you want for yourself. This can be quite painful, as it forces you to recognise that you haven't had the balls to take control of your own life. If, that is, you are self-aware enough to notice.

This can be why we often can't seem to stomach people who are assertive and say what they want. It makes us realise how shit we are at doing the same thing ourselves. Because, deep down, we know life would be simpler if we all just said what we wanted: no crossed wires, no misinterpreted words. All that saved time!

'She knows what she wants – and she told me!'

Damn ... just imagine it for a second. Doesn't that feel like a nice, clear space to be in? A simpler world?

In some ways, and I hate to use this wording, 'I want' can appear selfish. And I don't mean that it's bratty or spoilt. I mean that it's so bloody unheard of, in this day and age, for someone to take control of their own life and unapologetically say what they want, that it can seem somehow selfish.

But it isn't selfish. It's IMPORTANT.

When you work on bettering yourself, it can, indirectly, make others feel crap.

Why? It's not as if you have done anything to them personally. But it can, whether consciously or subconsciously, make them realise how much they have been shitting on themselves their entire life. They get defensive that you're changing things first, not them, so they make out that what you're doing is self-centred.

You need to get OK with that.

Your desire for getting what you want out of this one little, very short life we lead has to come first. Other people's feelings, which you have no control over anyway, come second. If you're not OK with that, you may as well stop reading this book now, because you will forever be living your life for other people. #sorrynotsorry

It forces you to take centre stage

Saying 'I want' forces you to confront those deep inner desires and lay it all out on the line. It's vulnerable. It leaves you feeling naked and open.

I vividly remember when I was making music for a living, my manager asked me what I wanted to achieve in the long term. In my head I could hear a voice saying 'I want to be the next Pharrell Williams. I want to be the female Dr Dre. I want to work with the world's best rappers and have everybody in their cars bumping my tracks!'

What did I say out loud?

'I just want to make enough to live on.'

Wow, what a fucking underwhelming response. Looking back, I want to shake myself. No wonder he wasn't excited to push my music. How could he buy into the vision when I couldn't even communicate it myself?

You know why I couldn't communicate it?

I literally felt stupid to be thinking in that way. I felt like it sounded silly and childish and pathetic. I could almost imagine him turning around and saying, 'Whoa, there, all right, love, let's just make a track first, shall we?!' – even though he'd never said or expressed anything to make me think he'd react like that.

I was worried about what he'd think of me. I wasn't

worried that he would think I didn't have vision for the future or a long-term plan, or any of those MORE IMPORTANT things. I was just worried he would think I was stupid for dreaming that big.

It upsets me now to look back on how stifled I was: how scared I was to admit what I wanted. I had a really promising music career and I know that if I'd stuck at it, I could have been the next Pharrell, but I could never ever admit it to myself, let alone speak it out loud. The words would not even come out of my mouth. It's like when you fancied someone when you were younger and everyone knew it, but instead of proudly admitting you liked that person, you'd take every possible opportunity to rubbish the idea. You'd say, 'As if!' and list every single flaw they had, just to prove how much you didn't fancy them (although I'm sure all this ever did is confirm just how much you actually did). Then you'd go home and write their surname after your name night after night in your journal.

CONFUUUUUSING!

Admitting what you want forces you to take centre stage.

You must be courageous.

You must confront every little voice that tells you that it is stupid or lame to want what you want, and you must say it out loud. Even if it's in a quiet voice. Even if it's mumbled and rushed out so fast you barely even have time to take stock. The important bit is that it gets out there: out loud. Speak the things you want into existence. Say 'I want', then finish the sentence.

Keep doing this until you run out of things to say!

At first it may feel a little weird. You may feel guilty, you may feel selfish, you may start reeling off wants that are not for you but for family members, because it feels like the right thing to do. Remember: this is just for you.

So, what do YOU really want?

COURAGE VERSUS CONFIDENCE

Some people wrongly assume that, in order to say what you want, you must have some innate, born-with-it confidence. Not the case. In fact, I believe that confidence is a by-product of courage.

Read that again.

Confidence is a by-product of courage.

Courage is about bravery and a willingness to take risks. Courage is about doing something that scares the shit out of you, because you can see that there is something bigger at play that could be yours if you could just take those first steps.

Courage is about being frightened and feeling like an utter loser but doing it anyway. Courage is what people should really be waxing lyrical about; because people aren't born confident, but they are born with courage.

Confidence is a learned behaviour. A secondary behaviour, or a result, if you will.

It can only exist once you have personally taken a step

forward, done something 'out there' and then realised it went OK. Then you get confidence. Confidence is like a shiny, flameproof suit that you can only put on once you've already jumped over the fire. Jumping over the fire in the first place takes courage. Being courageous is doing something because you know it's going to be good for you, even if you don't quite feel ready for it yet. You make the jump, you get the suit. Every jump after that isn't quite as daunting, because now you have your cool, shiny, flameproof suit.

You must, must, must find the courage – not the confidence, because that comes after, but the COURAGE – to say what you want, out loud.

Finding this courage will bring more money, more opportunities and more abundance.

So, in what ways can you foster a sense of courage in yourself?

Look at the bigger picture

In the moment, the fear of doing something outside of your comfort zone (like proudly declaring how much money you want to make next year) can overwhelm you so much that the reason you're doing it, the 'why', can fall into obscurity. We get so caught up in freaking out about the thing we have to do that we can forget what the 'doing it' results in.

It results in the thing we want to happen actually happening!

Right now, as you're reading this book, I'll make an assumption that your bigger picture is wanting a wealthier life for yourself: one with more financial freedom, where the topic of money feels fun and light instead of stressful and heavy.

The momentary embarrassment or cringe-making moment of speaking out loud about what you want will pass; focus on what it will bring your way. Think about the end goal: more money and more life!

You MUST get past this initial worry and have the courage to get real with what you want. Your life – and financial situation – absolutely depend on it.

Realise that people forget about stuff pretty fast

Often when we lack courage, it's due to the fear of failure: of publicly fucking it up and being left vulnerable, open for people to pick at. Maybe you don't currently feel strong enough to withstand any kind of picking. Fair enough, mate. I don't know your life story, but I do know that finding courage is one of the hardest things for people to do. I'm not saying it's easy for anyone.

What I will say is that people move on from things pretty fast. As they say, today's news is tomorrow's fish-and-chip-shop paper. We humans have a constant need for more news, more gossip, more events, so when you're in the thick of laying out what feels like a BFD (Big Fucking Deal) to you, like finally admitting you are sick of being in debt and want to clear that debt within twelve months, it can feel like the world's eyes are on you.

'Did you hear what she just said?! She wants to clear her debt in twelve months? As if! Didn't you see that she just bought herself a new dress? And she'll have to stop getting so many takeaways if she wants to save anywhere near enough money.'

This is the story we create in our heads.

The reality is that some people will think things like that. Some might even say them. But you know what? Who cares? By tomorrow, it's old news. They will have moved on to the next person, the next story, the next drama.

People who react like that aren't the people you need in your life – and you most definitely do not need to give a whiff of one shit about what these people think or say.

You are on to bigger things.

What's the worst that can happen?

Be real with yourself. When you sit down and think properly about the worst possible scenario of what could happen if you find the courage to talk about what you want in life, is it even something that would realistically happen? This applies not only to talking about what you want in a monetary sense, but anything. How often do you play over all these potential bad outcomes in your head?

'Jane might think I'm full of myself.'

'Annie will think I'm too big for my boots.'

'They will be sitting around talking about me at their next dinner party and I won't be there to defend myself.'

NEWSFLASH. This shit is not actually worth worrying about. This is not the same as your house burning down or someone you love dying or the rapid decline of the planet. No. This is not any of those things.

Hell, this isn't even as bad as being stung by a wasp. But for some reason, our brains like to think it is. Because, OH GOD, NO! THE WORST THING IN THE ENTIRE WORLD IS PEOPLE NOT LIKING ME!

The worst that can actually happen is really pretty minor. Someone might say something about you, or someone might *think* something about you. When we stop and logically take a look at the worst that could happen, we realise it's usually pretty stupid to worry about it. Your mind is taking something super-small and turning it into a catastrophe.

Let them talk. Did I mention that YOU ARE ON TO BIGGER THINGS?

What's the best that can happen?

Something that my money coach, Jen, drilled into me early on was the habit of asking myself, 'What's the best that can happen?' It's so at odds with everything we ever learn to think. It's so at odds with how the majority of society thinks.

Because – shock, horror! It's positive! And you'll start to see that positivity is NOT the norm. I mean, when is the last time someone asked you, 'What's the best that can happen?'

Asking yourself, 'What's the best that can happen?' allows your mind to be free. It allows you to dream about the way things could go if you just relaxed into it. It lets you think about all the great and brilliant and wonderful things that are actually a possibility, even if you believe they are just a dream for now. That's OK; allow yourself to dream it.

If you can envision a scenario where only the best outcomes happen, even if it feels pretty far from reality, that's good. It means you have the potential. That potential is what's going to take you from being someone who believes they can only make £30k a year to someone who believes they can make £300k a year.

So, go ahead. Ask yourself: 'What is the best that can happen if I talk about what I want?'

Perhaps someone, somewhere, will say, 'Oh wait, I could help you with that.'

Maybe it will help you to feel more courageous because you took a stand for something that you really want, which will lead to improved confidence.

Maybe, if you believe it, the universe listens. And maybe, just maybe, the universe delivers.

ALLOWING YOURSELF TO GET WHAT YOU WANT

By now, I hope that you are starting to see that it's OK to know what you want. It's even better to know it and say it out loud. Knowing what you want does not make you a bad person. If you still feel like it does, I'd suggest asking yourself this:

Who in my past has made me feel bad for saying what I want?

In the same way that confidence is a learned behaviour, so is shame. If you have high levels of shame around speaking up for what you want, it's likely that somewhere in your past you have been shamed for doing so.

Try and reflect on where this shame has come from (or, should I say, *who* it has come from) and understand that their shaming of you says a lot more about the type of person they are than it does about you. People who shame others for speaking up for what they want often do so because they can't find the courage to speak up for themselves.

It's a protective layer: a projecting layer. *If I can't fix myself, I project my bullshit on to other people.* On this path of self-discovery, you will often see this behaviour rear its ugly head. But not for you!

Shame is a powerful emotion, and it has no place on your path to manifesting the money and life you want. You want to get to a place where no one can make you feel shame for what you want or for being open about it.

What I'm talking about here is allowing yourself permission to go for what you want. To speak about it. To shout about it, even! I am at a place in my life where I proudly proclaim what I want to anyone – and everyone – who will listen. In fact, I have a big long list of things I want. I talk about them quite openly and, if you follow me on Instagram,

I'm sure you will have heard me waxing lyrical about them many times.

- I want to go to Palm Springs.
- I want an MBE.
- I want to make a million.
- I want to make money faster than I can spend it.
- I want to send my daughters to private school.
- I want to go on a romantic holiday with my husband at least once a year.
- I want to take my whole family on a luxury, all-expenses-paid holiday.
- I want to build a business that changes lives and becomes a household name.
- I want to be on TV.

How does that feel for you to read? Do you find yourself thinking, 'God, she's so brazen!'?

GOOD. Get used to it.

I *love* telling people about my ideas. I see it as reinforcing the power of these ideas and making them more likely to come true. I know that the more I speak about something, the more people I tell about it, the more likely it is to happen.

Do you know what happened as soon as I started saying these things? Shouting about them? Telling anyone and everyone I met that this is what I wanted?

They started to happen.

Not only did things start to happen for me, but people

started telling me that they had been motivated to start saying what they really wanted, too. People who followed me on Instagram started sending me DMs telling me how I had helped them to open up new parts of their life, to face parts of themselves that they had never wanted to face, to get real with what they really wanted out of life.

All because I had simply said what *I* wanted. I believe you have a duty, especially if you're a woman reading this, to speak out about what you want from life. Not only will the honesty of it help you find peace and strength; it will help others, too.

Here's why speaking your wants out loud makes them more likely to come true.

It's a commitment

People often won't share what they want or say it out loud because it becomes a commitment. This has both a positive and negative effect, depending on the lens through which you view it.

Negatively, people can shy away from commitment. You may think, 'I don't want to say I want to go on holiday this year because if I don't, people will think I've failed.'

Fear of failure is a massive part of this. We don't like to share things that we might fuck up: that's natural. It's a defence mechanism to avoid criticism and scrutiny. In these days of 'the highlight reel' and Instagram perfection, it's rare for people to talk about failures, at least not in a way that has no flip side to provide clever reflections. We might hear people talk about a failure that actually taught them the biggest lesson they'd every learned, which then led to them creating a million-dollar company. We rarely hear, 'Yeah, I just screwed this up because I prioritised going out and getting drunk over knuckling down and doing the work,' with no positive outcome on the flip side.

Saying 'I want this' not only makes a public declaration. It also means you hold yourself accountable. And if any part of you doesn't want to do the work or doesn't think that you can achieve it, you'll find yourself chickening out of sharing it: it's a clear sign!

A commitment can be a very positive thing. So, are you willing to make the commitment to yourself to make it happen?

Now, let's get into the whole commitment and account-ability thing. I don't think it's an area we talk about enough. We often don't see something we have worked on as having any merit unless it has been externally verified or certified. We need to have someone tell us how great we are before we believe it ourselves.

Do you know how crazy that is?

In order to achieve anything written in this book you must become someone who can self-verify, self-congratulate and hold yourself accountable. It's important you commit to something because YOU want to do it.

This commitment is one of the reasons that saying what you want out loud works. If you're serious about holding yourself to something and not failing, making a commitment out loud can be positive and motivating. After all, letting other people see you 'fail' (if it even comes to that) might feel shit, but failing yourself should feel a thousand times more shit.

Consciously, you don't want to flop yourself. But subconsciously, something about saying what you want out loud helps it to sink in. Your subconscious brain will begin working towards making it happen, finding ways to bring opportunities to the forefront of your mind. It'll start creating ideas or working on the problem long after you close your eyes to go to sleep at night.

Getting your subconscious mind on board with what you want is one of the ways to make it happen even faster, as it won't want to let you down.

You're less likely to give in to failure

We're busy people, right? At any one time we are likely to have a shitload of stuff going on. From kids' birthdays to friends' weddings, home purchases, career moves and every other little thing that fits in between.

This busy-ness means it's pretty easy to cop out on commitments, especially if no one ever knows these commitments existed in the first place. You just blame your colleague adding her workload on to yours, or your five-year-old coming home with a head full of nits. If you've never outwardly spoken about your aims, you've never committed to them, and if you haven't committed to them, giving in to failure is way easier because there is no one there to hold you accountable. It's easy to let it slide.

'Go easy on yourself!' you might say. 'You just had to spend the whole evening picking nits out of your daughter's hair, so you don't have time for that thing you never actually told anyone about anyway!'

This is where you need to use your fear of failure, and your fear of what people might think or say about you, to your advantage. If I've said something out loud and I've told people about it, as hard as that may have been, I now know it's out there. I know I've told you previously not to give a shit about what people think (and I stand by that) but if there is a time and a place for that, it's now: use that worry about what people think of you in a way that actually serves you. If you're worried that other people will think of you as a failure if you flop on the goals that you've been talking about, guess what? That might actually stop you flopping.

*Plays *The Twilight Zone* theme tune.*

THE UNIVERSE CAN HEAR YOU

Finally, I believe that, when you speak about what you want, the universe listens. There is no fancy, psychology-driven explanation to this one: just many years of observation. Whenever my subconscious wants and desires have been out of alignment with what I'm *saying* I want, nothing has happened. It's as if I've stood still. If anything, more crappy stuff has happened: things that I in no way want.

In the world of spirituality, it's often said that the universe hears without detail. So, if you are constantly saying, 'I don't want to be poor,' all it hears is 'poor'. Whereas if you focus on what you DO want, e.g. 'I want to be rich,' it hears 'rich'. And delivers.

As I said, there is no explanation for this, nor is there any way to prove that it is true (or not true). After all, there is no 1800-ISTHISWOOTRUE? hotline and I can't find any scientific studies to prove the magic, but it is supported by positive psychology.

All I know is that saying 'I don't want to be poor' creates negative emotions and feelings of lack. Focusing on the flip side, the positive way of saying it – 'I want to be rich' – keeps you in a more positive mindset. You're thinking about how things could be, not how you don't want them to be.

The way you speak and the language you use have a very strong influence over your life, whether you believe in the power of the universe or not. In the next chapter, we're going to delve deeper into which words and language will have you feeling like a freshly blow-dried, affluent, bad-ass bitch.

❦ *EXERCISE* ❦

To end this chapter, I want you to get really clear on your wants.

Once you write down what you want, say it out loud or tell someone. You are making a commitment to yourself. So, here's what I'd like you to do:

1. Think about what you want.
2. Write it down somewhere. If it's somewhere you will see it quite often, like on your phone screen-saver or inside your knicker drawer, then you get extra points!
3. Say it out loud or tell someone who can hold you accountable. Make it real!

CHAPTER 4

STOP TALKING SHIT

I used to think that, if I wanted to make £100,000, I simply needed to strategise and work out a plan for how I could hustle my way to getting those one hundred thousand sweet-ass British pounds in my account. When I thought about it, I saw action, energy, wheeling, dealing and working my ass off. If I'm honest, the energy that I associated with making that money almost seemed like it would feel quite exploitative. It also felt strangely masculine. Maybe I still associate making top dollar with being a dude, but that's for another session with my psychoanalyst.

None of my thinking about making £100k involved me focusing inwards or reflecting on the kind of mindset I'd need to have. It was all outward. What could I sell? Who could I sell to? For how much?

This makes logical sense, right? You want to make money? Well, then, you need to work out how to make it! That was what I thought.

Now, I'm not saying that working out the logistics of making money is not part of it. But it's not the most important part. The most important part isn't talked about that much, because it can be really fucking hard. Almost harder than the actual going-out-there-and-hustling part.

But I can guarantee that the hustling won't work unless you do this first:

Focus inwardly.

Let me fill you in on a well-kept secret about making money. The amount you can make is directly affected by what you *believe* you can make. It sounds so airy-fairy, right? A fluffy statement. But this, my friends, is some deeply profound shit. And this deeply profound shit is step one towards reaching the money you want to make.

Step one is convincing yourself that you are the type of person who can make that kind of money. It's about starting to *believe* that you can do it. Yep, you. You deserve – and can have – that £100k (or whatever number it is for you).

This is where our subconscious blocks and limiting beliefs can come into play, because, no matter how much we might be able to visualise our future wealthy life, or envision ourselves in ten years' time on a yacht in the Mediterranean, if your subconscious is going, 'Nah, mate, don't believe it,' then it isn't going to happen.

Time and time again I have seen this happen, not only

to myself but to the many business owners and creatives I work with. The easiest way for me to demonstrate this is with pricing. I know a lot of small business owners and some of these are service providers. I often look at their pricing structure and pull them up on the fact that they're not charging enough for their services. I don't just mean that they're not charging enough by the market rates, but also that they're not charging enough based on the value I can clearly see they are adding to their clients' lives in doing the work they do. But I'm often met with resistance about increasing prices. 'My client won't go for that,' they say. What they really mean is, 'I don't believe that I can charge that much. I don't know if what I offer is good enough and I don't want to piss off my clients by increasing my prices because then they will really start picking through what I'm doing and realise that it's crap. I am crap.'

I've heard this from many people, and I have never once thought that anything they were doing was crap – I'm sure none of their clients did, either. But this lack of belief in themselves and what they can charge is prominent. It's a funny thing, money. It has an energy, whether you're talking about it, spending it or owing it. It has some mega-force energy that is hard to put into words, but you just KNOW what I'm talking about. The hold it has over you when you owe someone money, or the joy you feel when you have enough cash to pay your bills and still have some left over to treat yourself to something. Money has got some serious big-dick energy.

Maybe it's because the world and society as we know it

is built on money. Who knows? But because that energy is there, you need to harness it for your own good. You must train yourself to believe that you are a person worthy of money, and that you *can* get the money you want.

In a recent conversation with a friend, we talked about how I wanted to turn over £400k in my business in the coming year. I vividly remember coming to the realisation that there was no point in us sitting down and mapping out how, practically, I would do it.

Instead, what we needed to do was start working on my belief that it *could* happen. That I was the type of person who could have a £400k turnover business. How did we do this? Two simple steps.

We worked out why I felt it wasn't possible. In my case, it just felt like more money than anyone I'd ever known – my parents, grandparents, friends – had ever earned. I didn't know anyone 'like me' who had made that kind of money, so it didn't feel real.

Armed with that knowledge, I started researching people who *were* 'like me' and who *had* created businesses with that kind of turnover. Other mums on Instagram, influencers and people from humble backgrounds. That helped me to see that it was possible for them, so it could be possible for me, too. After all, why was I any different?

Sometimes, you just need to find some evidence. Once you believe something is possible, the vibe changes.

You tell someone your price confidently and they immediately accept.

You have a deep feeling that the amount of money you want to make is possible, and it happens.

You get the pay rise at work that you now believe you are entitled to, because you finally, and confidently, ask for it.

It's a strange, something-in-the-air feeling that can't be explained when someone confidently believes that something is possible. You just naturally believe in them too. They attract your confidence and your trust.

On the other hand, when someone doesn't believe in themselves, you can get a sense of it immediately. It's a whiff of desperation, of inauthenticity, and something just feels 'off'. It doesn't matter whether that person is in front of you, on the phone, or even on TV: if they are talking a number that, deep down, they don't believe they can get, you can pick it up instantly, like a bloodhound picking up on the faintest of scents. You call BS.

I don't want that for you. I want you to believe in yourself and to be able to get the money that you came here to get.

It won't be an overnight process. Personally, I had to go from being someone who was making £20k a year to being someone who believed they could make £50k, then £100k, then £200k, and so on. I'm still on that journey (and I'm still working on the belief that I can have a £400k turnover business).

Luckily for us, our brains are not hardwired. Thoughts, beliefs and even behaviours can change easily, thanks to a little something called neuroplasticity. Neuroplasticity is the ability of the brain to rewire itself at any chosen moment.[4]

Imagine our brains are like a huge field. Across this field there are various paths that have been trodden that help us get from one area to another. We know these paths well, and they're easy to walk because we've trampled down the grass a million times before. These paths are called neural pathways. They can be seen in the way we form thoughts and beliefs, and they create our behaviours, too. For example, if I have gone from one side of the field to another, via a path I always take, and I've been able to get food from one side and bring it back, I'm going to have a pretty strong belief that, should I want food, that's the path I need to take.

However, should we choose to give it a go, new paths can be trodden down to create new neural pathways at any time. If I challenge myself to find or create another path to the food on the other side of the field, I can probably do it. It might be more challenging because the grass is longer and the route is unfamiliar, but I can give it a try and see what happens. If I get to the other side and successfully collect the food, then I know that I could take this path again. The more times I take the path and tread down the grass, the easier it gets to follow. Over time, the old path starts to grow over, until it barely exists anymore.

It's not always that easy. Sometimes I might find myself going back to the old pathway as if on autopilot: we revert to old behaviours or thought patterns out of habit. However, if we continually take steps to make our new neural path-way the norm, eventually it'll become second nature. This process is neuroplasticity.

The way we do something can be changed. We are changeable. IT'S SCIENCE, GUYS!

REWIRING YOUR BRAIN

The first time I ever experienced neuroplasticity in action was when I changed my beliefs around money. Since then, I've been a lot more malleable in my approach to many things and it's had positive effects across various areas of my life, from dealing with anxiety to improving my fitness and even how I eat. So, trust me, if you can learn to rewire your brain to believe you are worthy of having more money, you can use it for a hell of a lot of other things that will benefit you, too. Get ready for being YOUR BEST SELF.

Ready for treading down some new paths?

Here is how to change your old, limiting beliefs into new, positive beliefs around money and more.

Your language

Negative language is destructive. Speaking negatively, or in limited terms, especially about money, does three things:

- it reinforces to your subconscious that what you want to achieve is 'not possible';
- it stops any potential external positive involvement; and
- it attracts other people who talk in the same way.

Now, I hope the fact that you picked up this book means that you'd like to attract more opportunities and money into your life. I also understand, however, that you may not yet be at the point of believing that that can be possible. It's all well and good to sit back and say, 'I want to make a million quid.' If your subconscious doesn't believe it's a possibility for you, it's just not going to happen. As you're probably starting to realise, your subconscious mind and your conscious mind need to be on the same page.

Language is the easiest place to start. After all, most of us spend a large portion of our day talking and it's therefore a tangible thing to notice and change fairly quickly.

But why are the words we use so important? When it comes to communication, don't body language and the unspoken elements really make the difference?

I know it can seem that way.

Often, when getting into long, drawn-out arguments with my husband, I like to remind him of how important his body language is.

'Why did you pull that face when I said that?' I'll ask him.

'What face? I didn't pull any face,' he'll respond.

I'm sure we've all been there: someone is saying something, but their body language doesn't quite match up. Something about the vibe is just *off*. A subtle eye roll, crossed arms, a sigh. My husband likes to tell me to focus on the *words* that he is saying, not the way in which he is saying them. 'But 80 per cent of communication is body language!' I cry. He's a logical man, so he likes to keep it simple: 'I said this, therefore that is what I meant.'

I wish I could feel the same way.

For some reason, in the heat of an argument, all of my clever wording goes out the window and I end up in a flaming ball of hyperbole, emotions taking over, no thought before the words fall out of my mouth, causing way more damage than intended. I'm an emotional person and, when it comes to many things in life, I rarely think before I speak.

However, one thing I have noticed is that, when it comes to reprogramming how I talk about money and opportunities, I am a *master* at wording. I think before I speak, I am self-aware, I am eloquent and positive. This isn't something that I was born with. It's something I've learned.

Before, I used to talk about money and opportunities in the same way that I speak during arguments with my husband, in a mass of emotions and exaggerated claims. I'd say things like:

'I'll never be able to buy that.'

'I'll never be rich.'

'I wish I could afford it, but I'll probably be poor forever.'

I was playing the role of a victim. I want to go back and shake myself! You see, your words have more power than you realise. They not only have the power to influence others, but they directly influence your own subconscious, too. Constantly reinforcing any doubt or lack of belief with your day-to-day language can set you back on your journey to subconscious belief in your goals.

To understand how our words can influence our subconscious, I spoke to Jacqueline Hurst, a certified life coach, clinical hypnotherapist and Master Neuro Linguistic Programming practitioner. Jacqueline says:

What you think about expands, and how you talk to yourself really matters. Neuro Linguistic Programming helps you understand that the 'map is not the territory'. In other words, your internal thinking determines how you view life, but it might not be reality.

Beliefs really matter when it comes to life results. A lot of the time, our beliefs are distorted, generalised or simply limited. If you need to change your results, you have to start by changing your thinking.

If we mistake our subjective and possibly distorted view of reality for reality itself, we become hindered, frustrated and stagnant. Not a pretty look! Ultimately, we all have a different way of doing things. For example, if you ask a botanist, a homeopath and a chef the question, 'What is mint?', you will get three totally different answers. So, the way you view the world might not always be reality. Understanding the language that you use with yourself is the first step towards changing your life.

That little voice inside – you know, the one that talks at you all day? Well, that is the voice you need to get under control. Just like a puppy in training, it is time to train your mind.

First, it is a good idea to work out any primary thinking errors you may have. For example, are you catastrophising? Are you mind-reading? Are you projecting? Are you treating your thoughts as facts?

Secondly, ask yourself this: are your thoughts consistently negative and limiting? If so, it is time to change this. The power is all in your hands: if you change the way you look at things, the things you look at change.

Understanding that you are completely in control of your thinking is empowering.

As an example, if you are saying to yourself, 'I must make more money', it feels heavy. Changing that language to 'I *can* make more money' already feels better, right? Or you could be saying, 'Money is hard to come by.' You can change this language to 'Money changes hands every second of every day – it can't be that hard to come by.' This feels almost exciting!

When you say negative things to yourself, like 'This is impossible' or 'I will never be able to do that', you could start looking for evidence to disprove these thoughts. Find evidence to prove why something *is* possible, or why you *are* able to do that. Using positive evidence to disprove and break up negative thoughts is such a powerful tool.

Understanding how you organise your thinking, feeling, language and behaviour is imperative if you want to start achieving the results you are looking for. Start by thinking about what you are thinking about. What you think generates how you feel, how you feel generates what you do or don't do, and what you do or don't do generates your results. It starts and ends with your thinking.

The power of positive language is nothing new. We hear about how important it is from athletes, world explorers and people facing challenging situations every day. But why is it that telling ourselves something as simple as, 'Yes, you got this, girl! This is piss-easy!' helps us so much more than saying, 'Bloody hell, this is hard work. I'm so tired. I don't know if I can do any more'?

Positive words are words that allow for things to happen. They have potential; they open our brains. Negative words are limiting. They are closed and final. Not so great if we are trying to open ourselves up to the idea of having more money!

If you're trying to psyche yourself up to run a marathon, you'd hardly start the race by saying, 'Hey, you know what, Sarah? You can't do this. You might as well just stop now. It's hard, there are bumps all over the road and your feet are already hurting. What's the point?'

You've already decided on the outcome, and the outcome seems bad. In response, it's likely that your body would start to feel sluggish and want to give up sooner.

Compare that to telling yourself: 'This is gonna be easy! I feel light on my feet and I'm ready for this challenge!' You would probably find that your body could go longer, push itself harder and want to make it to the finish line.

If you've ever been at the gym, you'll know the difference between how a workout feels when you're in a positive mood versus a negative one. A positive frame of mind is everything. And there is growing evidence that language and motor experiences are linked in the brain.

In 2012, a study was done to investigate whether motor skills – in this case, a person's grip – would be influenced by positive language.[5] The participants of the experiment listened to 'action target words' spoken in either affirmative or negative sentences while holding a sensor in a precision grip. What the scientists found was that, shortly after hearing an affirmative or positive sentence, the participants' grips would have more force, but when they heard the negative sentence, no changes were observed. The positive sentence the participants heard was, 'At the gym, Fiona lifts the dumbbells.' The negative was, 'On the plane, Laura doesn't lift her luggage.'

This is one of the first research studies into the effect language can have on the body, but its results are pretty striking. If we can see that speaking positive words can affect our physicality, what can this do to what we believe we can achieve?

The annoying thing about language is it's so habitual. It may take you a while to start catching yourself using negative language around money. It's not always as obvious as a friend asking you out for dinner and you saying, 'I can't do that, I'm too poor.' It can sometimes be more subtle, such as agreeing to go to the dinner, then sitting down, scanning the menu and saying, 'Ahh, that lobster looks amazing! Wayyy too expensive, though.'

See what I mean?

It can creep in easily without you noticing. This is not only due to our own language habits, but those of our friends, too. Hearing something talked about as being 'way too expensive' seems quite commonplace, doesn't it? Sometimes things really are expensive, but you do not need to voice these concerns. The sooner you notice any sort of negative or limiting statements coming out of your mouth, the sooner you can change your language. You'll start to notice when you are fishing for sympathy or being overdramatic. I believe that language is one of the first and easiest ways to change your money mindset almost instantly.

You might be wondering how you can change phrases to be more optimistic rather than limiting. Here are some examples that personally worked for me.

CHANGE THIS TO THAT

Change: 'I can never make that kind of money.'
to: 'I look forward to the day I make that kind of money.'

Change: 'I can't afford it.'
to: 'I'm not spending in that area at the moment.'

Change: 'Ahh yeah, that looks nice. One day!'
to: 'Ahh, that looks nice. That'll be me soon!'

Now, when I speak about things I want, opportunities and money, I speak in positive terms. I leave statements open-ended, full of potential.

Even if you're thinking something negative or limiting, don't say it out loud. Imagine that whatever you say out loud is exactly what will happen. Imagine it's like sending out an intention to the universe that says, 'Give this to me'.

If you say things like, 'I can't do that, I'm broke', then damn, girl! You just made that shit come true. The universe is like, 'You're broke? GRANTED!. Imagine the universe is like a stupid dude who also has shit hearing. It's like when you yell down three flights of stairs to your husband who is going to the shops: 'WE DON'T NEED ANY SUGAR, BABE!' What he hears is: 'Mmppfhhhh pmmhffff sugar, babe.' So, he goes to the shop and happily brings you home a bag of sugar, so pleased with himself that he got what he thought you wanted. But you know how you could have avoided this? Don't tell him what you *don't* want. In fact, don't even use words that are the thing you don't want. Just focus on what you *do* want. Make that clear in your speech and put it at the forefront of your mind. Anything you talk about is like you putting in an order to the universe for it to happen. So, it makes sense that we want to keep saying positive things rather than making definite statements about our current shitty financial situation. It will just keep you there.

Now, I'm not going to lie, it can be really hard at first to keep your language optimistic. You want people to understand that you are working your ass off for sixteen hours a day and still don't have enough money to get a takeaway.

I GET IT.

I get it because I was there. It can be hard to switch off the language that attracts sympathy. But it just makes you a victim. And being a victim will *not* get you financial abundance.

If you are feeling like stuff is hard, I'm not saying to suppress your feelings. Just be real with yourself about why you want to say it. If you need to talk about it, try saying to a friend, 'Can I talk to you? I feel really pissed off at the moment. I'm working my ass off and I want more recognition for it, financially and personally. I know I am destined for more.'

What did the universe hear?

I want more recognition.

I know I am destined for more.

Keep it simple. Try to frame your language in a way that allows room for growth and space for opportunity to arise. Don't make statements that come from a limited mindset. It may take you a moment sometimes to work out the right thing to say. Even now, I still have trouble sometimes, and YES, I still make mistakes! Just say to whoever you're talking to, 'Hold on. I'm trying to work out how to word this in the right way.'

It becomes a fun game after a while. I mean, my idea of fun used to be hanging out smoking weed and chatting shit at squat raves till 4 a.m. Now my idea of fun is catching myself using negative language. God, I'm getting old!

Other people's language

Another point on the whole chatting shit thing: even once you are starting to master the skill of using positive language, it can be easy to slip back into old habits. I have noticed it is easiest around MOANY MATES. Once you start figuring out how you want to talk, you will begin to notice how many Debbie Downer mates you have who just *love* to moan about money.

It can be really challenging to be the odd one out who starts talking in less limiting terms. You will notice how negative and limiting your friends' language is. They will probably notice the change in you, because it's out of character and a new pattern. They may tease you about it. Stay strong. They might not be ready to change their financial situation yet, but you are. Over time, when they start seeing your new optimistic outlook on life, they may start to change their behaviours too, but that's for Chapter 10.

You will even start to notice negative language when you meet new people. I spot it in an instant – and I often correct them! Not in a negative way, though. I'll say, 'Hold on, you're fucking amazing – OF COURSE you will be able to go on that holiday soon.' I find that women are especially hard on themselves, for fear of coming off as 'too big for their boots'. Do yourself and the other women in your life a favour. Teach them how to talk themselves up instead of down. Show them how to use language that is open instead of closed. Pull them up on their victim statements (but say it nicely, as no one really likes to be told they are playing the victim). Give them an example of how to rephrase what they are saying. (You can do this with your kids, too. It's important to teach kids about positivity around money – but perhaps that's another book!)

TAKE A COMPLIMENT

How you respond to compliments is another area where I see people constantly self-deprecating (not, as I once proudly proclaimed in an interview, self-*defecating* – that would just be weird).

It's important that you learn to take compliments. I often say, 'Wow, you did such a great job,' to a friend, only to hear, 'Ahh, are you sure? I think I messed up that part.' I want to shake them! Accepting compliments is a huge part of building your self-worth and confidence. Plus, being able to accept compliments exudes a form of 'Yes, I know I'm the shit, mate,' that has everyone bowing down.

Can you imagine paying Beyoncé a compliment and her saying, 'Oh, I dunno, I think I kind of sucked'? Nah, mate. Wouldn't happen. She knows she's shit-hot – and you should too.

The language you use in the conversations and statements you're putting out into the world is important, and it's of equal importance to be able to *respond* positively to comments and compliments that you receive. Don't talk yourself down or make yourself 'lesser than'. 'Lesser than' people do not make money. Do you know who makes money? People like Beyoncé. In fact, I can't think of a single person I know who makes good money and has a 'lesser than' mentality. They all know how great they are, and they BELIEVE in themselves. If you can think of someone who is 'lesser than' and still makes dough, I would imagine they are the rare exception and by no means the rule.

HOW TO ACCEPT A COMPLIMENT

'Thank you!'
   So easy, but so hard to execute.
   Give it a go.
   'Thank you.'

Just say that, then stop. Ban yourself from following up with a self-deprecating statement. It might feel uber cringe at first, but before you know it, it becomes second nature.

In fact, all of this language stuff becomes second nature. I'd say within a few months, you won't even believe the crap that used to come out of your mouth. You'll hear people with limiting beliefs talk in such closed and negative statements that it will make you sad for them, but also bloody grateful that you learned to sort it out.

I really feel like this alone could change the world. #dramatic

¥ *EXERCISE* ¥

Use the space below to record any negative language you hear yourself or others around you using.

_____

_____

_____

_____

_____

_____

Try to catch yourself when you use limiting talk. If you have a friend who is on the same wavelength, you could hold each other accountable by checking in daily to see if you've managed to keep any negative money talk out of your speech. Once this is at the forefront of your mind, you will find it easier to change your habits!

£

CHAPTER 5

GET SOME PERSPECTIVE

Get some perspective. It's something I say to myself when I can feel I'm getting too caught up in a situation and need to give it the bird's eye view. Stay neutral, stand back, take your emotions out of it.

Perspective is interesting. It's how we interpret people, things or events around us. It's how we understand things, relative to *our* world. Our little bubble that we live in inside our own heads. Because we all think that the way we see things in the world is how the world actually is: the reality. Heads up – it's not. It's just your perception of it.

What *is* reality? We each have our own versions of events: our personal beliefs, past experiences and pre-conceived notions create the world that we believe to be reality around us. For example, if, as you were growing up, everyone who you encountered that had money was greedy and selfish, you may well have gone on to keep this as your preconceived notion of how people with money will act. I, on the other hand, may have had a completely different experience. The wealthy people I had met might have been kind, charitable, selfless and generous. It doesn't matter how many times I tell you that your perception isn't correct: to you, it is the utter truth. It is your own reality. It is your world.

One of the most helpful things you can do for yourself is realise that your world does not equal anyone else's world. Once you understand this, it can help you across many areas of your life. You may even find it easier to relate to your partner or children. For example, my perception of my daughter constantly interrupting my conversation with a friend is that she's trying to wind me up on purpose, whereas my daughter may feel like she's being ignored and that I'm more interested in talking to my mate than I am in spending time with her. If I can understand her reality before getting annoyed, it could help me be a bit calmer, and even lead to better communication and love between me and my daughter.

We've all heard the saying 'There are two sides to every story'. For ages, I interpreted this as 'there are two sides to the story, but only one of them is real – and the one that's real is *my* version of events'. It can be painful to admit we're not always right and that there might be people out there who just have a completely different way of seeing the world.

Perspective is all about how you interpret things that happen. For example, you could find yourself stumbling across some lost cash while reading this book. One perception of this might be that it's just coincidence. And one might be that you are getting a sign from the universe that you're on the right path.

When Jen and I run our Money and Manifesting course, within just a couple of days we start getting stories from students who have found money. Often, they have stumbled across a twenty-pound note on the ground outside, someone offers to pay for their lunch or they get an unexpected refund. It's always so fun to see the ways in which money starts turning up in our students' lives. At first, it seemed so strange that this was happening every time we ran the course, and to what seemed like a large percentage of the students. How weird that it was all happening at once: these exact people, in this exact group, at this exact time, all having the same good luck! Incredible!

The magic of this money just appearing for our students intrigued me quite a bit.

I do believe that there is something about group energy and a 'high vibe'. High vibe describes anything that feels good in your soul and body, lifts your spirits and comes from a place rooted in love instead of fear. On some level that I can't explain, I feel like there is an element of magic at play when a group gets together, all sharing this high vibe. The universe could be helping us along the way of starting to believe in the power of manifesting by conveniently dropping money outside our front doors – throwing us a bone. Sometimes, when you ask for a sign, you get one.

Or, is it more that when you *look* for a sign, you get one? Because asking for and looking for are two very different things.

Our brains like to go to work and do what we tell them. Was the money on the floor that our students found always going to be there? Would it have been there, regardless of them asking the universe for money to be attracted to them? Would they have even noticed it, had they not attuned their minds to look out for money being attracted to them?

If I asked you to go out and notice how many magpies you see on your travels today, I'd imagine you'd spot a fair few (unless you're reading this from, I dunno, Bali, in which case, your wildlife may be pretty different). Or if I told you to go out for the day and count how many yellow things you see, you'd be surprised by how many you noticed.

You'd probably think, 'Wow, I've never noticed so much yellow stuff before!' For some reason, today the world seemed full of yellow things. Or maybe the world *is* full of yellow things and you've only just realised? Maybe it's a coincidence?

COINCIDENCE AND SYNCHRONICITY

Coincidence is defined as 'a remarkable concurrence of events or circumstances that have no apparent causal connection with one another', and 'the fact of corresponding in nature or in time of occurrence'.[6]

Coincidence is such a strange thing. Although it is a natural occurrence, it can also be so remarkable that we sometimes don't quite believe it. Two seemingly unrelated, random events that just 'clash' and share their magic at the same damn time. Weird, huh?

Many people argue that there is no such thing as a coincidence. They might say, 'God, it is so fucking weird that I've bumped into my ex *three times* lately. It just *cannot* be coincidence – and it was right after I had been talking to my friend about how I was thinking of calling him. There must be something bigger at play here. It's a sign. Maybe we should get back together.'

I don't know where I stand on this. Is it the universe at play? I do like to feel as if I'm being guided, having little signs thrown at me to help me along with my decision-making or life moves. You might have experienced those moments too, feeling that signs from the universe are guiding you in a certain direction. But my science brain also kicks in here. Did the girl *want* to see her ex? Did she have him on the brain, so that, on a normal busy street where she otherwise may have walked straight past him without realising, she happened to spot his face among the crowd?

Do our brains just like to construct stories around chaotic events that make no sense, simply because we like the idea of order and feeling as if we have some control over our lives? Will we ever truly know if this is magic or plain old scientific coincidence?

In the 1950s, Swiss psychiatrist and psychoanalyst Carl Jung came up with the concept of 'synchronicity'. He described it as 'a meaningful coincidence of two or more events where something other than the probability of chance is involved'.[7]

I take his phrase 'meaningful coincidences' to mean 'when things could have happened by chance, but it doesn't feel that way'. Synchronicity is when an occurrence feels like it was arranged by some bigger power. It has more meaning than a coincidence. It's like an orchestrated coincidence that has meaning, but only to you.

An example of synchronicity could be the girl above, who bumped into her ex-boyfriend twice in one day and wondered if this had a bigger meaning. To anyone else it might be a coincidence, but to her it's 'a sign'. Another example could be people who believe in numerology suddenly seeing 11:11 all the time. Weird fact: just as I started writing this chapter, guess what I started seeing everywhere? 11:11.

Us seeing something as 'a sign' is what Carl Jung was getting at in his synchronicity theory. It's the search for meaning in coincidences. The search is being carried out by our subconscious.

The subconscious can attempt to bring emotions to the surface by creating a feeling of meaning in connection to what could just be a natural coincidence. That doesn't mean this feeling should be ignored: quite the opposite, in fact. I would listen up, friends. If you start to see 'signs' or synchronicities, I would pay attention to them. They are likely to be your subconscious giving you a gentle (or sometimes quite obvious) nudge in the right direction.

Now, I love a spiritual, magical moment as much as the next girl, so I'm not going 'debunk' tarot or mediumship or psychic readings, but if you are the type to be a little sceptical or want to know the science behind things, just know that, for many people, something like a tarot reading can be an act of synchronicity. Its meaning is derived by the reader through the use of symbols and explanations. It's likely that, if you are a sceptic, you would not find anything meaningful in a tarot reading. If you're not a sceptic, though, and you're looking for the reading to work, you will find meaning and resonance in it.

Simply put, we can manipulate our minds and our beliefs to work for us. You can choose what to believe in and you can choose whether something has meaning. I would suggest that, if something gives you a positive, high-vibe feeling, you should allow yourself to believe it.

Just because something isn't proven doesn't mean that it won't work.

If we come back to our example of the girl who saw her ex – let's call her Natalie – it's likely that Natalie still has feelings for her ex and wants to explore the idea of them getting back together. Her finding meaning in the coincidence of them bumping into each other (or is it a coincidence at all?) is the validation she needed to explore this idea, even if only in her head or in a conversation with a friend. It may end up that she doesn't ever get back in touch with him and decides that she did the right thing by splitting up with him. But the subconscious brain wanted to explore it further, so it found ways to make her do so.

I know that sometimes things can just be *too* coincidental. Crazy shit, beyond even synchronicity. I remember I once wrote down a list of things I wanted to happen over the coming months. One was to work with luxury fashion brand, Moschino. Now bear in mind that, although, yes, I can be deemed an 'influencer', I am by no means a fashion influencer. In the years I've been doing brand collaborations, I've done about three fashion ones, in comparison with probably hundreds of interior design collaborations. They are rare, because my scope is more in entrepreneurship, interior design and parenting. But when I went to sleep after writing that down, I kid you not, I woke up to an email asking if I wanted to do a collaboration with Moschino. The exact brand I had written down just a few hours prior. I couldn't explain it.

Here's another example. Recently I spoke to a friend who had had a hefty tax bill show up. She had most of what she needed saved, but it was £6,000 over what she had. I had a conversation with her just after she had found out and, naturally, she was a bit worried about finding the money she needed to pay the bill. She resigned herself to working extra hard and scrimping for a few months to get the money together. But she also put it out to the universe that the £6k would show up. She just asked for it: visualised it coming to her and the tax bill being cleared. Within an hour, I had another call. My friend had quoted £4k to a brand who were interested in collaborating with her on a project. She said they had come back to her offering her £6k instead and saying they would pay it in full the following week. I can assure you; I have never heard of a brand offering to pay more than the quoted fee AND offering to pay in full. Usually it takes a load of negotiating to get the fee you want, often followed by months of chasing for payment after the work is complete. My friend got the money she needed to cover her tax bill and she got it fast. Again, it couldn't be explained.

TOO WEIRD. I don't think I can explain this away. Could it be coincidence? Maybe. But, wow – what a coincidence.

These occurrences do keep me with one foot in the world of magic. Sometimes there is no other way to explain something other than to say, as famed author Gabrielle Bernstein says, 'the universe has your back'.

Our perception of events like these is that we have had a sign from the universe. Asking for a sign, then getting one come through to you can be very powerful indeed. Whether it truly is the universe answering you or your subconscious reading events in a certain way, does it really matter? As long as you get to where you need to go, right?

Can you think of a strange coincidence that has happened to you lately? Write it down below. What meaning, if any, did you give to the coincidence? And since reading this chapter, could it be perceived in any other way?

_____

_____

_____

_____

_____

_____

ATTRACTING GOOD OR BAD FORTUNE

We have all known that person who seems to just inherit bad luck. They appear to be a victim of a terribly unfortunate set of circumstances, and, no matter what happens, they just can't catch a break. It can be horribly upsetting, traumatising even, and to some it can be a life-long cycle that never breaks.

When I worked in retail, I had a boss who always seemed

to have one drama or another on the go. You know the type? One weekend she had been up all night arguing with her boyfriend, so couldn't come to work. The next she had food poisoning. Then there was a fight with a colleague ... it went on and on, until finally, she was sacked. During the small number of shifts we shared together, all I heard her do was complain and moan about how dreadful her life was and how many shitty things happened to her on a regular basis. Every time I saw her it would be another story of hardship, but not in a genuine way. In a long, drawn-out, blame-everyone-else-for-your-problems way. She made me want to crawl away and hide in the changing rooms under a big duvet, protected from her negative fucking energy. Just thinking about her now makes me feel crap.

I don't know what was going on with her behind closed doors. Well, I mean, in some ways I did, because she laboriously dragged out every monotonous detail, but I didn't know what was *really* going on, inside her brain. Did she grow up unloved? Did she desperately need attention? Did something about being a victim gave her a high?! Who knows – I'm no psychoanalyst. But, fuck me, there was clearly some shit going down.

It can be hard to spend time giving love and energy to these people because they are seriously draining; they squeeze every little bit of positivity out of a situation and have a way to close down any suggestions you make to try and make things better. They have a 'no' for every possible solution.

Makes me shudder to even write about it. But we've all known someone like that. Maybe we ourselves are that person or have been at some time.

I'm going to say something quite controversial here. In some cases – not all, but some – I feel like these people can attract bad situations. Before you jump down my throat for being insensitive towards people with problems, hear me out. There are, of course, genuine victims. People who have experienced horrible tragedies that could not have been stopped, no matter what. I am *not* talking about those people.

I am talking about the people who play the role of victim throughout their lives, no matter what the circumstance, no matter how privileged they are or what good things come their way – because often, bizarrely, there are a lot of opportunities for good stuff coming their way, but they overlook them. These people attract more negativity. Here's why.

The idea of 'attracting' something is, in my mind, all about perception.

If you tune into all of the shit stuff that happens to you each day, without spending any time focusing on all the great stuff that also happens to you each day, it will mean your perception of the world, day to day, is negative.

It's just like putting on a pair of glasses with a blue tint. The whole world around you will look blue. If you spend all your time focusing on the negatives without forcing yourself to also address the positives, your perception is skewed negatively. Some people also call this a 'lack mentality', which, in theory, means you see everything in terms of what is lacking rather than what is in abundance. It's the whole glass half full, glass half empty thing.

People can 'attract' bad things into their lives because they simply perceive things in that way. When you focus on bad things, you get more of the same, because your brain is tuned into focusing on negative elements and so looks out for more.

This lack mindset might not apply across all areas of life. For instance, you may have an abundance mentality when it comes to love and relationships, but a lack mentality when it comes to money and finances. The end goal here is to get you to having an abundance mindset in the area of money. Hell, my end goal is to get you to have an abundance mentality across all areas of your life, because I promise you, you'll see the results. But let's start with money, hey!

Whether you are indeed attracting something towards you due to the Law of Attraction or whatever else is not for me to say. As with coincidences, sometimes it's just too weird to explain. But I do believe that if you go looking for something, you will find evidence of it. If you perceive everything that happens as negative, you're likely to see more negativity. Your brain will filter out all the good stuff, because it doesn't fit in with your preconceived notion of what's going on.

HOW YOUR PERCEPTION AFFECTS YOUR MONEY

Once you understand perception, you can use it to your advantage. Perspective can be manipulated to work for you: to change your beliefs, to help you be more positive, or even to help you feel like you're attracting money.

So, how do we start the process of changing our perception, and therefore moving from a lack mentality to an abundance mentality?

Our brains love to decide on something, then look for evidence to support it. This can happen even if the things that the brain has decided upon are COMPLETELY FALSE. We call this confirmation bias.

Our subconscious wants to find repetition and patterns to predict what will happen next. All it wants to do is create a cosy little space in which you can stay safe, and it does that by looking for evidence to support a belief we already have: 'I've seen this happen five times, so now I believe it to be fact.' Perhaps you were spoon-fed some of this so called 'evidence' by people like your parents when you were growing up, so their perception of the world becomes yours. Our subconscious mind creates these little patterns to keep us safe, because trying to think situations through without these instincts or beliefs in a fast-moving world like ours would take too long, and could, in theory, put us in danger (real or perceived).

Confirmation bias can be great when something that could put us in danger starts to happen. If you are in a dark alley and see someone creeping around, your confirmation bias would probably kick in and tell you that it's likely something bad might happen, making you move out of that spot pretty sharpish. If you ignored your confirmation bias and spent time trying to think it all through logically, you might be too late to avoid the danger and the worst could happen. So, it has its plus points.

The problem with confirmation bias is that it can take over and start looking for evidence to support a belief that is not true or doesn't serve you in any way.

We disregard any contradiction of what we believe. We ignore the pattern that's out of sync. We ignore the customer who says she doesn't like the taste of our brownies because *we've* tasted them and think they are incredible. We decide she must just have a poor palate.

As you can imagine, this kind of thinking can lead us way down the garden path and could result in some bad decisions being made.

We see this in politics all the time. If we have decided we like a politician and what they stand for, we could be presented with an incredible amount of evidence to disprove our beliefs about them, yet we will ignore it. We will believe positive stories about our candidate and ignore negative ones, putting them down to the other party being wrong. What is more likely is that you and your chosen candidate do have some different perceptions of right and wrong, different perceptions of the world, differing viewpoints, but your confirmation bias is leading you to stick with your guy, despite what comes up.

Our brains are stubborn little things. We rarely challenge our own beliefs, because to do so is uncomfortable and scary. Deep down, it feels a bit unsafe. Because if we're wrong about this, what else is happening in the world that we're wrong about? Nah, we don't wanna hear it.

When it comes to how we think about money, confirmation bias shows up often. Once we have a set belief about money, we are likely to defend it until the end. But I know from experience that it is entirely possible to change your beliefs and perceptions. And negative money beliefs will not help you make more money.

So, how do we avoid confirmation bias affecting how we think about money? We have to disprove the theory or belief. Scientists do this to make sure that they are not unintentionally manipulating results to fit their preconceived notions of what the outcome of an experiment will be. In Chapter 1, we started to look at our negative money beliefs. Now we are going to start trying to shift them to change our perception.

DISPROVE YOUR NEGATIVE MONEY THEORIES

There are three steps to starting to disprove your negative money theories:

1. Look for evidence.
2. Stay in dreamland.
3. Keep track of your progress.

Look for evidence

First, you need to recognise what your negative theories around money are. Your answers will be individual to you, but some common ones I see are:

- Money is evil.
- People with money are greedy.
- More money, more problems.
- You have to work really hard to make money.
- Someone like me could never make a lot of money.

Compile a list of your own negative money theories, then we can get to work. All you need to do now is start researching. For example, if we take 'people with money are greedy' as an example, you would then go looking for examples that disprove this theory: people who are very wealthy, but also very generous. You can use YouTube, Google, social media and other platforms to search for examples that disprove this idea. After all, it is a huge, sweeping generalisation – but I'm sure, by now, you are already starting to see that.

Start putting together your evidence document. You could do this in writing or by collecting pictures. Now, every time you start to hear the 'rich people are greedy' thought come into your head, you can look at all the examples of people you found who are *not* that way. Of course, there will be some rich people out there who

ARE greedy. That's just life. But there will be plenty who aren't. You are training your mind to wear a different set of coloured glasses: a colour that sees money in a positive light, not a negative one.

EXAMPLES OF HOW TO DISPROVE SOME NEGATIVE MONEY THEORIES

Money is evil
Find as many instances as you can of large amounts of money being used for good.

People with money are greedy
Find examples of rich people who have been incredibly generous with their wealth.

More money, more problems
Think about times when you yourself have had money and found it to be useful, not problematic or stressful. Journal about those moments.

You have to work really hard to make money
Think about a time when you have made money from doing something fun. Or think back to a time that you have had money show up easily for you. Perhaps a gift, an unexpected win, a job that ended up being

way easier than you thought it would be. Again, journal about those moments and how you felt. If you can't find personal examples, ask friends (not negative ones!) or other people for their stories.

Someone like me could never make a lot of money
Find examples of people from the same kind of background as you who have gone on to become wealthy.

It really doesn't matter if these people or situations are the rule or the exception. We are not trying to win a Nobel Prize here! What you are trying to do is create new neural pathways in your brain and remove any form of confirmation bias you have around money. We are trying to find positive associations and examples to disprove your theories, so that your brain can start realising that money can be a positive force in your life – and that *you* can be someone who has it, perhaps even easily.

At first you may find you feel some resistance towards this activity. Your mind will start to find lots of reasons why it's rubbish. You will come up with stories or excuses about the examples you have found: 'Well, they must have had some help,' or, 'Well, they are the odd one out – most rich people aren't like that.' Don't worry – this reaction is very normal. Just work through it and treat this exercise as an experiment you are running on your own mind. The aim of this book is to change the way you think, and to change your own behaviour. That won't happen if you talk yourself out of it or look for evidence of it not working – that'll just be your confirmation bias at work once again!

Stay in dreamland

Another thing you can do to start changing your perception of money is to follow the rule 'ignorance is bliss'. I know that this saying is often used in a negative way, but we are using it for good here, people!

While you're challenging your beliefs, shifting your perception and trying to create new neural pathways in your brain, you have to protect yourself a little. It's easy to fall back into bad habits or negative thought patterns, which can lead to an overriding lack mentality, so we want to do our best to avoid that.

While you're trying to disprove your beliefs about money, you need to ignore any opposing views. This may be tricky at first, as you'll start to see how 'normal' it is to talk about money in a negative way, and you'll notice how much of mainstream culture is based around the theory that money is evil. You will need to go on a diet of sorts, to cut out the opposing views and train yourself to focus only on the positive money conversations that are happening.

I have been doing this work for so long now that I can hear opposing views and they won't sway me off course.

I can listen and provide counter-arguments, or listen to people who have different points of view without them influencing me. But it took me a while to get there, and it took a long time to educate myself and disprove enough of my bullshit negative theories about money to be able to hold my own in those conversations. Because, trust me, if you start cutting out people with negative views, or begin using only positive language around money, you're going to be challenged on it. It will be tough to stand your ground and stay on course, but it's important if you want to become someone who makes money.

How to cut out opposing views, at least until you have forged some new neural pathways

- Stop following people on Instagram who are negative about money.
- Change the channel if you see money being portrayed in a negative light on TV.
- Hang out with the people who fill you with hope and excitement about money, rather than those who pull you down.
- Don't read the newspaper.
- Read books that tell stories of positive money experiences and skip out anything that's focused around the negative aspects.

Keep track of your progress

While you are undergoing this important transformation of how you think, it's important to document every step of your progress. In doing so, you'll keep your newfound money positivity front and centre. And, as we all know, where focus goes, energy flows! Keep your eyes on the prize.

At first, you might just pay attention and observe when you have had negative thoughts, used negative language or made a passing negative judgement. Take a moment to stop and observe. I find it quite enjoyable to start doing this, as you realise your brain is like a little monkey who wants to keep playing. You can act as the responsible adult who just sits back and observes its wildness. Once you have got used to catching yourself in a negative money spiral, you can change your thoughts. Go back to your list of evidence that disproves the theory and remind yourself of the positive money associations you have.

You can also keep track of all positive money experiences that happen to you, or that you witness happening to others. Perhaps it's being gifted a coffee, finding money on the ground in the park, seeing a friend get an unexpected tax refund or seeing someone you follow on Instagram making a living by doing what they love. Use these to build up your own collection of evidence that disproves your negative money beliefs.

A great way to track your progress is to ask yourself at the start of each week to give a rating out of ten for how you feel about money, with one being terrible and ten being great. Over time (and yes, it may take some time), you will see the needle start to shift. I'm not saying that you will never encounter challenges around money, but what you will start to notice is that, the more you focus on the positives and train your mind to change its perception of the world, the easier you will find it to deal with the ups and downs that every single person goes through with money – and yes, even rich people experience these.

Documenting your progress and the incredible things that you start to notice happening to you will help your mind to focus on the positives and create new neural pathways. Before you know it, you'll be feeling like a money magnet.

£ *EXERCISE* £

For a few days, look and listen for representations of money around you. Train your brain to find it wherever you go. It could be on a billboard or a magazine cover; you could see stacks of cash in a kids' cartoon or over-hear the word 'money' in someone else's conversation on the train. Notice how it seems to be all around you once you shift focus and pay attention!

In the space overleaf, record any positive money experiences that happen to you or other people around you.

_____

_____

_____

_____

_____

_____

You can download a PDF worksheet to help with this chapter at www.themoneyiscoming.com.

$

CHAPTER 6

PULL YOUR FINGER OUT

Right, guys: you've read through the previous chapter and, by now, I would assume you have a pretty good understanding of what's going on deep inside that slimy little brain of yours.

At the halfway point of your *The Money is Coming* journey, let's take a quick recap.

In Chapter 1, we learned about how the world around us has been programming our minds to feel negatively about money since birth. Whether those influences came from our parents, things we've seen on TV or how our friends feel about money, they have been there all along, providing thoughts and actions that may not even be our own. Ultimately, these influences have not been helpful in our quest for creating and receiving money. From this, we now understand that the beliefs that we had taken on could have been holding us back from attracting more money.

In Chapter 2, we explored how our judgement of others and deep jealousy of what others have has been holding us back from really bringing money into our own lives. We learned that, in order to start welcoming good fortune and wealth, we need to halt any passing judgement around how other people earn and spend their own cash. Have you noticed that you've 'checked yourself' on your passing of judgements lately? We might not catch it every time – after all, we are all human – but it feels so much better when we reserve judgement, doesn't it? Much lighter, I think.

In Chapter 3, we got real about what we want, and spoke those wants out loud for the very first time. We learned that, by speaking or writing down our wants, we are triggering our subconscious brains to help us bring these ideas into fruition, because the subconscious is an absolute sucker for an idea. You should now have a clear vision of what you want to be, do and have, and may have already started visualising those things being a part of your life.

In Chapter 4, I showed you that it's possible to change how we think and create new neural pathways using only our language. Simply by changing our wording and avoiding any negative talk, not only with our friends but with ourselves, too, we can avoid perpetuating the lack mentality. How has your money talk been lately? Have you managed to catch yourself speaking negatively and switch what you were going to say for another, more positive phrase?

In Chapter 5, we got to understand how confirmation bias can stop us taking the steps we need to take towards a more abundant life. We discussed how we can influence and manipulate our own perceptions to work for us for the better, by removing confirmation bias and taking steps to disprove the stories our minds have made up about money. You might have started compiling evidence to break some of your negative money beliefs.

In this chapter, I want to talk about some of the 'Law of Attraction' type stuff we see out there.

Visualisation is often linked to the Law of Attraction because it provides a way for you to 'project' yourself mentally into what you're trying to attract. But I think there is a further step you can take. I want to talk about the art of combining visualisation and action, and how I believe that, if used together and correctly, they can really be the 'secret sauce' to attracting money.

VISUALISATION

Visualisation is the art of creating a mental image of something. If I ask you now to close your eyes and imagine standing barefoot on grass, you could create a visualisation of it. You'd see your feet nestled into the soft, green grass underfoot. Everyone's visualisation of this will be different. For some, perhaps it's sunny. Others may imagine a cold, damp day. Some of you could see male feet, others female;

you may see painted toenails or a toe ring. You may experience the 'feeling' of the grass underfoot differently to each other. There is no one correct image to visualise: the art of visualisation is simply to bring the mental picture to mind. If you did it, well, waheyyy! Congrats – you just had your first visualisation!

Visualisation is key to having money flow your way. You need to become someone who can visualise yourself in the financial position you want to be in in the future.

Every time you perform a visualisation, you are helping your subconscious bring an idea into reality. The more you go through the motions inside your head, the more the idea you are visualising feels like reality, or at least something that *could* be a reality. And that's the important part: letting yourself get to the place of believing it can and will happen.

Visualisation can have this effect in our brains, because our minds don't necessarily know the difference between what's happening in real life and what's imagined. We've all had those dreams where we are asleep but have felt like we are falling off a cliff. It makes us jump so much that we wake up. Or when you could have sworn you were holding an object, only to wake up and find there is nothing in your hands at all, even though it felt so real.

In some ways, the brain is getting primed for real life during the act of visualisation. This can impact cognitive processes in the brain, such as perception, planning, motor control and memory. It's quite incredible, really. Not only can our brain run through things that we have experienced and felt before, it can also do something quite extraordinary: it can visualise things that we have never actually experienced.

I know that visualisation has worked for me before, but I wanted to see what the science was behind it, so I went digging to see if anyone had done any studies on visualisation.

In a 2015 study, researchers found that a guided imagery technique that involved a combination of multiple senses and emotions was of greater benefit than one that only implemented visual images.[8] The study explains that, if you imagine an orange – not only the visual appearance of it, but also the texture, smell and taste – it can set off a physical reaction in your body. Whenever I am trying to explain just how strongly the visualisation technique affects the body, I only need to mention the word 'porn'. People quickly realise what the physical effects can be when we think about something that we find pleasurable, like sex.

The reason it's important to link the physical and mental connections of what we visualise is that it makes them feel more real. The problem with the Law of Attraction and starting to think and believe that you can be someone with money is that it can often feel like you're imagining someone else, or that it can't be possible for you. Visualisations, especially those that encourage you to use all five senses, help you to convince your mind and body that this is, in fact, a potential reality, because you've been there and experienced it before, even if only in your mind.

HOW TO PRACTISE VISUALISATION

Here are three different ways you can practise visualisation.

Create a mental picture

Simply close your eyes and try to envision a situation, environment or object. I find it helps if you think about how things around you may feel physically, or if there are any sensory connections you can make: sounds, smells, tastes. This can make the visualisation feel a little more real and help you get into it.

Try it now!

VISUALISATION PRACTICE

Close your eyes and imagine you are holding an object. Think of something that has quite a strong image, texture and smell, such as a cup of coffee.

First, think of the environment that you are in with this cup of coffee. Are you at home? In a coffee shop? In the park? Imagine what that environment looks like. What sounds are going on? Can you hear the noise of a coffee machine, the chatter of people or the sound of birds chirping?

Next, look down at your coffee. What kind of vessel

is it in? A paper cup from the coffee shop? A hardy earthenware mug? How does it feel on your hands? Is it warm? Next, imagine the aroma of the coffee wafting up towards your nose. Then, take a sip. What kind of coffee is it? A flat white? An espresso?

Just by completing this small visualisation, you should see how easy it is to create an incredibly vivid mental picture involving many of your senses.

Once you can visualise objects, you can move on to bigger things: houses, distant places and more. Anything you can find to help you make your visualisations more vivid is good, so feel free to get on YouTube and watch videos of places you'd like to visit. This can give you an idea of the sorts of sounds you would hear, for instance. If you'd like an incredible Malibu beach pad, look at images and videos of similar properties to the one you want for yourself. Pay attention to the details: what kind of fabrics are used? What is the daylight like? How do the waves sound as they lap at the shore? Then, set about visualising yourself inside that space: walking around, making a cuppa, wrapping a blanket around you as the sun goes down. The more detail you can add, the better!

Feel the emotion

You can also try and imagine the emotional reaction you may have if your visualisation was real. For example, I remember once I was nominated for an award when I first started my blog. I REALLY wanted to win. In the lead-up to the awards ceremony night, I would close my eyes and run through what I wanted to happen on the night, over and over again. I pictured myself having my name called, people clapping and cheering and the rush of adrenaline and excitement I would feel when it happened. I imagined myself walking up to the stage, thanking the host and smiling at the audience. Not for one second did I let myself explore the 'what if it doesn't work out?' scenario. I just stuck with the visualisation and the feeling of excitement about winning.

I won the award that night, and it played out almost exactly as I'd visualised. The feelings of excitement, the rush of adrenaline, the unashamed pride in myself ... it was all exactly the same as what I had been visualising.

I want you to try doing an emotional visualisation.

EMOTIONAL VISUALISATION PRACTICE

Close your eyes and imagine that you have just received a letter to say that you are owed £10,000, and there is a cheque enclosed for exactly that amount.

Don't start to question why or how this may have happened, just go with it! You've received an unexpected £10,000 cheque that you can put into your account and spend however you like, RIGHT NOW.

In your mind and body, let yourself feel the emotions that would go along with this. Would you feel crazy excitement? Relief? Pure joy? Would you scream and run around the house?

Sit with these feelings for a few moments. Let them wash over you as if it's happening, right now.

Create a vision board

Another great way to practise visualisation is to create a physical thing to look at to kickstart your imagination.

At the start of every year, I sit down to create a vision board of what I want. Some of my past vision boards have included materialistic stuff, such as cars, bags and outfits. They've also included experiences, such as beautiful places I want to travel to. I often stick on pictures of role models, such as people whose careers I admire. In the past I have included pictures of happy babies, to signify the calm and healthy births of my children, and magazines that I want to be featured in. I even had 'getting a book deal' on one of my vision boards – and here we are now, with you reading my words as a published author.

Vision boards provide a physical tool to help you visualise your goals in life. Position your vision board somewhere you will see it often, like inside your wardrobe door or next to your bed. Before you know it, your brain will go to work figuring out how you can make these things a reality.

Here's how to make your own vision board! You simply need a range of old magazines, some scissors, a glue stick and an A3 or A4 piece of card. You will be creating a board which has images of all of the things you want to 'be', 'do' and 'have' in life. Some examples might include pictures of destinations you want to visit or the kind of house you want to own, an image of a happy family, or pictures of people who look successful to you. It's hard to specify what you should choose, because each person is different. What success looks like to you may be entirely different to what it looks like to me. So, look through the magazines and start cutting out images that you feel drawn to and which represent the things you want in your life.

Stick these images on to your vision board. It really helps if you write annotations in the present tense as well. For example, if you stick on a picture of the Italian coastline, you may annotate it with 'I travel to beautiful destinations with my friends and family'.

A few tips:

- Try not to double up on images. It's better to keep your board minimal but punchy, rather than having five images that all kind of represent the same thing.
- Give your board a timeline: is it one for this year only, or is it one for five or ten years' time, that you will keep for ages?
- Once complete, put the board somewhere you will see it daily. The more it goes into your subconscious, the better! I like to put mine inside my wardrobe door so I see it every day when I go to get dressed.
- If you know you will be making a vision board in a week's time, start looking out for images that catch your eye in advance. If you can't find them in magazines, feel free to print out pictures of what you want. You can also make your board digitally using an online tool like Canva – but be sure to print it out and stick it up!

On my website, www.themoneyiscoming.com, you can also find a handy tutorial video sharing the best practices for putting a vision board together.

I've had so many things come true since putting them on one of my vision boards:

- getting pregnant
- getting my dream house
- brand partnerships

- a book deal (oh hey, reader!)
- holidays to particular destinations
- feelings I had wanted to experience, such as industry recognition or a freedom around finances

Saying this, I've also had my fair share of things I'd put on a vision board NOT coming true. And this might sound like a cop-out, but I can tell you why.

VISUALISATION ALONE WON'T WORK

I've often heard sceptics talk about the Law of Attraction as if you just stick a picture of a mansion on a piece of paper and wait for said mansion to drop into your lap. Or write yourself a cheque for a million pounds, sit back, put your feet up and relax. I think this can be a fair assessment, as often any talk of the Law of Attraction or manifesting lacks the depth or psychological information to provide any reason for how or why it works. I hope I can provide that here.

Visualisation is an incredible tool. It can turn what seems like a far-off dream into a reality, even if it is just for a moment, inside your mind. Visualisation alone can go a long way towards helping you feel more worthy of wealth. But it can't actually make that wealth happen. *You* have to do that – with a little help from the universe.

Using visualisation alone as a means to try and bring

more money into your life is only doing half the work. It's like having a car with no petrol, or a pancake with no syrup (a travesty, in my opinion). Visualisation must be combined with one very powerful force. It is this combination that will make all of the difference.

That powerful force is TAKING ACTION.

It's all well and good to sit at home and do your visualisations. In fact, I recommend that you practise your visualisations almost daily, maybe just before bed or when you first wake up, or whenever you have a spare five minutes. You'll be amazed at how much motivation you'll start to feel to make those visualisations a reality. In fact, according to the study on athletes and visualisation that I mentioned previously, using visualisation throughout their training was shown to help the athletes improve their focus and strength, and even their scores. But they couldn't *just* visualise themselves winning. They had to actually get off their asses and perform.

So now is your time to get off your ass and perform.

I'm so excited for you, because I feel like this moment, as you read this paragraph, is the moment we start to pull all of what I've been talking about so far into practice. It's where you're going to physically be able to see and experience the true manifestation of your goals. It all begins right now.

THE FIRST STEP RULE

Once, on a Skype call with Jen, we talked about how I would just love to take my family on a trip to LA 'one day'. Jen gave me what I now recognised as her knowing smile, with a glint in her eye that told me I was about to be schooled on something. 'By saying "one day",' said Jen, 'you aren't committing to this ever happening. "One day" is a way to put something off. How about you start taking action on this right now?'

I realised she was right. I had been putting it off because, somewhere in my mind, I didn't think it was realistic. Perhaps it would cost too much money; perhaps it was too big a trip to aim for at the point I was at in my life.

'How much are the flights to LA from London?' Jen asked.

'I have no idea,' I said.

'You haven't even looked into it?'

'No.'

'How about you start researching it tonight?' she said.

Jen went on to explain that, when you talk about the things you want to do and achieve 'one day', it's a way of keeping these ideas and dreams at distance. There will be an underlying reason why you're doing this: it could be a task that makes you confront something difficult about yourself; it could be a stretch financially; it could be something you know will take a lot of time, focus and effort. For instance, I have been saying for years that I wanted to write a book. It took me over a year to actually push myself to sit down and finish a proper proposal. Why? Because I knew it would be a big challenge, mentally, emotionally and intellectually. The point is, I was putting it off for a long time, until I decided to take the first step and put pen to paper for my book proposal.

Going to LA was like that. I had to take the first step. I took Jen's advice and I started researching flights, Airbnb accommodation, places we would visit if we went. I saved reviews and put alerts on flights. Doing this made it become REAL. Within a few months, we were booking a trip to LA for the first time ever. Various things helped it fall into place, all of which I am about to explain, but I can almost guarantee that if I hadn't taken that first step of researching the flights, even before I could think about how on earth we would afford it, I would still be sitting here now, saying, 'I want to go to LA one day.'

In fact, I've had a picture of Tokyo on my vision board for three years straight now. I still haven't taken the first step on that trip. I will sit and examine exactly why I haven't taken that first step privately, but I do know that, at the moment, it feels big and it feels scary. But I also know that, if I look back in five years' time and haven't yet visited Japan, I'll feel like a loser. I'll be that person who always has the dream but never takes any steps towards making it happen. I don't want that to be me and I don't want that to be you. Do you?

The First Step Rule is about taking what is a 'one day' idea and making it start to happen *today*. It is simply about taking one, real-life step towards your goal, whatever that may be.

When I decided I wanted to become a published author,

my first step in manifesting that becoming a reality was putting out an Instagram story in which I said, 'I have an idea for a book, and I am looking for a book agent. Can anyone put me in touch?'

Within hours, I had been sent a few names. I reached out to these agents and, of course, that set the ball in motion.

A lot of the First Step Rule is about research. Things can feel really 'pie in the sky' until you have solid research. Numbers, figures, contacts, emails. These things bring it from dreamland into real life. Not only do they give you the actual information you need to be able to take the next steps towards making it happen, they also give you a clear idea of exactly what you're working towards.

Once you have done the research and know what's involved in your goals, you will have a clearer picture. Your mind needs something to work towards. A next step, or a clear number that you need to get to. Then, lo and behold, it goes quietly to work in the background. The research step shows commitment. Not only to yourself and your subconscious, but to everyone around you, too. It's like the idea went from something that only ever existed in your daydreams to something that could – and is likely to – become a reality.

It also shows intent.

A lot of people talk the talk, right? 'I'm gonna do this one day, I'm gonna do that,' yada yada ... But we all know the people who talk all the talk, yet never – NEVER – actually take any concrete steps towards their goal.

It's like there's a little bell that goes off as soon as you start doing the research: DING DING DING! Hey, universe! Sarah finally pulled her finger out and started to research going to LA!

SHE'S READY!

It's like the universe was just waiting for you to get on with it the whole time. I believe the universe is like the wisest of parents. If I wanted my daughter to learn how to draw, I might pick up the pen, place it in her hand, then hold on to her hand while showing her how to move the pen across the paper in order to make a mark. If I did that, it's likely she would lose interest pretty quickly: after all, you can't force ideas on to anyone. You can lead a horse to water, and all that. But the universe is super-clever. It knows how to empower you to do something. It's not going to do it for you, but it can guide you and open up doors for you to help make it happen. It'll come along, leave a pen nearby, then wait to see if you go over to look at the pen, or even pick it up. If it sees you are interested and pick up the pen, it then may happen to leave a sketch pad somewhere for you to find, or it might put a show about learning to draw on the TV. Before you know it, the child has worked out how to use the pen, found the sketch pad and wow! What do you know? There is a TV show on right now about how to draw. What a weird coincidence!

The First Step Rule has never let me down.

I guarantee that, if I go and start researching flights to Tokyo for my dream Japan trip, within a couple of years of this book being out, I'll have gone. In fact, as a reward to myself for getting my book published, I might go and do just that.

TAKING INSPIRED ACTION

The essential message of this chapter is about taking action. But not just any type of action: inspired action.

Inspired action is what follows the First Step Rule.

Once you have taken the first step and done your research, you have made your intention clear to the universe and to yourself. You have committed to bringing what was once an idea into reality. Now, you might think that the next stage is simple. You do the research, then you act upon it. Right?

Say you want a pay rise, from £35k to £50k a year. Your first step might be looking up roles that pay £50k in your company. You may talk to colleagues who are making that as their salary, or you could look at job advertisements to get an idea of the sort of skills these roles require, so you can see if there's an area you need to work on. What is unlikely to happen (although notice I don't say it's 'impossible') is that you will walk into work tomorrow, sit down at your desk, and have your boss saunter over and say, 'Hey, Jade! I don't know why, but I couldn't sleep last night because I was just lying there going over what a great member of staff you are, and how unfair it is that you're only paid £35k instead of £50k. Do you know what, babe? I'm gonna offer you a pay rise.'

I mean, it might happen! I've seen some unexplainable shit in my time. But, in case it doesn't, we need to think about what comes after the First Step Rule.

We sit back and wait.

Yep.

Do nothing.

All you need to do now is . . .

OBSERVE.

You see, inspired action isn't about hustling to make something happen. It's not about force. It's not about controlling situations or manipulating outcomes.

It's about grabbing the opportunity when it shows itself.

Going back to my example of my dream trip to Tokyo. Some of you, after looking up the flights, might say, 'Screw it! Let's book it right NOW! And that might be totally cool. But if you start trying to 'force the issue', as my husband says, by maxing out credit cards or calling around family members to borrow the money . . . it's probably not going to work out how you want.

Why?

Forcing, controlling and manipulating outcomes is never a good look. This kind of action is aggressive. It is ego-based, and impatient.

Trying to force outcomes means that you create an expectation. That expectation can be tricky, because then you are not 'allowing' anything to just work out for you. You are trying to control it. It's also not in alignment with the positive 'attraction' vibe that we want to put out. We don't want to *force* stuff to happen. We want to *attract it to us*.

Would you like things to be hard, forceful and aggressive? Or would you like to have a more peaceful, fun flow of opportunities?

This can be a hard question for many people, because we are brought up in a society that teaches us that hard graft and 'hustle' are the only ways to get what you want. Over and over again, we are shown that, if something just falls into your lap, you haven't 'earned it' and you might be judged and chastised by society as a result. Just look at how we treat socialites or the children of billionaires.

Moving away from the idea of hustling and into the idea of letting things flow can be hard. I myself still have some resistance to this and, even after seeing it work many times over, I still feel as though I won't be respected unless I have worked my ass off for whatever I receive, be it money or opportunities. We worry that we won't be respected and that we will be judged. We worry that people won't be happy for us; that they will say we are just 'lucky' and talk about us behind our backs. And I'm not gonna bullshit you: that probably will happen. But if it does happen, it's because, deep down, we all just want an easy, fun life. And if people see it being fun and easy for you to make money, they might feel envious.

Inspired action is about jumping at opportunities when they arise. It's about being courageous and perhaps doing something that scares you or pushes you outside your comfort zone – but in an exhilarating 'this will be good for me' way, not a 'what the fuck am I doing, get me the hell outta here' way.

Moments of inspired action may feel like coincidences. It may feel like the universe is leaving you breadcrumbs leading you towards something that feels as if it was just 'meant to be'. But, over time, you will start recognising places where you can take inspired action. You will start seeing opportunities arise. This could be within days, or weeks or months, or, yeah, sometimes, years.

Let's say I go and research these Japan flights tonight, then in a month's time a friend of a friend mentions his dad has this amazing Airbnb in Tokyo. I WOULD NOT TAKE THAT AS COINCIDENCE. You get me?

Or say you want a pay rise but you're not sure how to make it happen, then one day in the shower you suddenly have the idea of putting together a document showing exactly how you have helped the company achieve its sales targets in the last six months, and what a valuable member of the team you are. For God's sake, make that presentation!

As soon as you open your mind up for new ideas and possibilities to arrive, you'll see that a little opportunity for inspired action will just drop into your mind.

Even when it doesn't quite go to plan, the universe, or maybe our subconscious, wants to keep us on a positive track. I believe it wants to help us along in making decisions that have a fun and happy vibe about them. But on occasion, even after following the First Step Rule and then seeing moments of inspired action, there can be less than desirable outcomes. When this happens (and it will, don't be shocked), pay attention to what can be learned.

The universe and your subconscious may show you things along the way. Sometimes they show you the same things over and over again. The universe likes to show you lessons: it likes to guide you. This might mean some stuff doesn't work out to plan. You could spend days, weeks or months whining about it and complaining about the world not being fair, or you can look at what the universe might have been trying to show you, what lessons can be learned, reflect on it and then move on.

So, listen to your internal guide. If you see little clues or strange coincidences start happening, pay attention to them. Act upon them. Whether they are synchronicities, the universe throwing you a bone or just a straight-up coincidence, who gives a fuck if they help you reach your goal?! Don't overanalyse it, just jump in with both feet.

Remember, inspired action isn't about *making* it happen; it's about *allowing* it to happen.

It's about an action feeling energising rather than draining.

It's about saying 'Yes' to the things that are going to be good for you.

It's about looking for the clues or little signs and saying 'Yes' to them.

Inspired action is about grabbing the opportunities and

coincidences that arise and saying, 'Hello, I see you! I want to be involved. I'm ready!'

$ *EXERCISE* $

Take one of the things you want to be, do or have, and put the First Step Rule into action. Write down some numbers, research prices, send that initial email, ask for help, do your research. Take the first step towards making your idea a reality, then sit back and wait for a chance to take inspired action.

€

CHAPTER 7

DON'T WORRY ABOUT IT

The irony of writing a book about money and calling a chapter 'Don't worry about it' is not lost on me. Indeed, money can be one of the most troublesome and anxiety-inducing aspects of our lives. Everywhere we look, it seems that money can cause or solve many problems that we face day to day. By no means have I been dirt-poor, but at moments I have suffered (as, I'm sure, has everyone reading this book), the waves of deep worry, stress, inner turmoil, frustration and resentment that a lack of money can bring, regardless of the actual figures in my account.

A lack of money can turn the sweetest of relationships sour. It can bring out a darkness in us, even anger. It can make us act out of character and it can change our view of the world. It can make us bitter, sad and depressed.

At this point, I just want to say I really feel you if you recognise yourself in any of those statements. I know what it's like to be there, and it's a huge deal that you have even picked up this book. You are taking a significant first step in starting to change the way you view money. If I've learned anything on my journey from bounced bill payments, thousands of pounds of debt and scraping by on minimum wage to having a six-figure business and a fantastic lifestyle, it's that money is one big game.

Mostly, it's a mental game, and once you start to learn the rules it all becomes a bit easier. I can't promise to make you a millionaire overnight, but I truly believe that if you take on board what I'm saying and really go through the self-reflection that is needed, the very notions of money and wealth will start to feel more fun, light and easy.

When I started working with Jen, the main feeling I remember having after each session was one of relief. Money felt like a huge burden, a tightness and weight on my shoulders. After each session, I felt lighter and more at ease with the phenomenon of money. I didn't get stressed out so easily, I could sit back and observe it, how it works and how the world and its inhabitants fall over themselves to command it. I felt more like an observer. I could see money for what it was and I could see how it had control over me my whole life. I could then start to make the necessary changes to my life. This was all down to a new perspective: a more detached perspective.

From reading the previous chapter, you will know about

the First Step Rule. You know you need to take your first step towards a goal, then wait for a chance to take inspired action towards making your goal a reality. This 'waiting' part can really piss people off. It can seem confusing, and it even feels lazy to some people, especially if you're someone who is a go-getter. For me to sit on my hands and wait for things is almost impossible. I'm a 'now, now, NOW!' person who does not deal at all well with the idea of delayed gratification. But, once you take the first step, the most important thing you can do is become detached from the outcome.

I know, to try and not care whether the money turns up or not can seem totally at odds with the idea of making money in the first place. Surely, if you have a goal, you want to work towards making it happen, right?!

We have been conditioned to believe that, if we want something, we need to keep it in our sights and hustle, hustle, hustle until it's ours. I'm not saying taking action isn't the right thing to do. By all means, if a series of opportunities that allow you to take *inspired* action pop up, then GO FOR IT. Go hard. Do great work.

But you must try to become relaxed and detached from the results of what you're trying to manifest. This detachment is the thin line between *wanting* something to happen and *needing* it to happen. It's the art of needing nothing but attracting everything. This is the bit I struggled with – and I *still* struggle with it a lot of the time.

THE ART OF NON-ATTACHMENT

'Detachment is not that you should own nothing, but that nothing should own you.'

—Ali Ibn Abi Talib

Non-attachment, sometimes referred to as detachment, is the art of being unattached to the outcome of something. It is practised in many religions and spiritual beliefs and provides a sense of peace: an escape from the uncontrolled restlessness that working towards a desire can create. It helps to create a calm, relaxed state, and a calm, relaxed state is where we are able to best manifest our goals.

When I first heard about non-attachment, I was at a local Buddhist centre. I had seen some evening classes advertised offering an 'Introduction to Buddhism'. I've always been quite interested in different religions or spiritual movements and how they see the world, so I decided to go along. Non-attachment is quite a big part of Buddhism, so naturally it came up within the first lesson.

'Non-attachment,' the teacher said, 'is when an individual can overcome his or her desire to be attached to things, people or outcomes.'

This seemed an odd concept to me. I mean, I can understand the whole 'don't be attached to material items' idea because, at the end of the day, it's just stuff (although I sure as hell am attached to the fifty-plus pairs of Nike sneakers in my downstairs cupboard). But aren't we brought up to understand and acknowledge the value of people in our lives? To love and care for them? Of course we're attached to people!

When I thought about the idea of losing a loved one, the ultimate in detachment, it brought tears to my eyes. As for many of you reading this, it's my worst fear. How could I practise non-attachment as a wife? As a mother? Non-attachment seemed cold and unloving: the opposite of how I want to be as a person and at odds with what I saw Buddhism as being about from the outside.

I asked the teacher about this.

'Non-attachment is not about being unloving or unemotional. We don't mean for you to be non-attached to commitments or responsibilities. Non-attachment is about not trying to control the outcome. It's about relinquishing attachments to preconceptions, to certainties, to your self-image. It's about accepting that life has its ups and downs, ebbs and flows, and being able to observe this and be at peace with it rather than trying to control things. It's about not expecting things in return for your efforts ... it's about loving without expectation, giving without expecting something in return, and being compassionate.'

I found this most interesting. For a while afterwards, I really tried to practise non-attachment. It's not easy: after all, we have been conditioned to feel that we can control absolutely everything in our lives if we just hold on tightly enough. But, as I'm sure you're aware, life doesn't always turn out as we had planned.

Trying to control and manipulate situations creates a false sense of security. It sets up expectations that, yeah, OK, *sometimes* work out – but when they don't work out, we often just CANNOT FREAKIN' DEAL!

When I tried to practise non-attachment, I felt more at peace with the ups and downs of life. I felt like more of an observer. Things didn't quite get to me as much; I wasn't as pissed off or angry when things didn't work out my way. I just sort of shrugged my shoulders and moved on.

Isn't that the dream? To just be able to shrug your shoulders and move on from something if it doesn't work out? After all, we know that dwelling in anger, resentment and pain is not high-vibe, dudes. And I want to be high-vibe! I don't want to be a Debbie Downer, do you?!

How non-attachment can help you manifest money

I'm going to give you an example of someone trying to make £6,000 to take their family on holiday. I'll show you the two different ways in which this can take place.

Example A shows what might happen to someone who hasn't discovered the principles in this book. Example B shows the experience of someone who has learned and is applying these principles.

Example A

Person A decides she wants to go on a dream family holiday. She thinks it's out of reach but writes it down as a fun 'one day' goal anyway. Person A looks at some holiday options on a package holiday website and gets a rough estimate that she'll need about six grand. Person A decides to go all in: she's committed to making this trip happen! She scrambles around trying to think of ways to find the £6,000. She decides that it's worth putting it on a credit card, because it'll be an amazing trip, and that way she can pay it off gradually over the coming months. She tries to put it on her credit card and realises that, unfortunately, she doesn't quite have enough credit left to do it. She is pissed off now. She had her heart set on this holiday and could have sworn there was enough on the card to cover it, but she'd forgotten about the car repair she had to charge to the credit card a few months back. By now, though, she's super-attached to the outcome – Person A WANTS this holiday. She and her family have discussed it, and she's not going to go without. She applies for another credit card, gets approved and uses it to pay for the holiday. Person A and her family go on holiday and have a fabulous time.

Example B

Person B decides she wants to go on a dream family holiday. The old her would think it's out of reach, but she decides she is going to stay open-minded, because she now knows that if she puts her mind to something, it can happen. She writes it down as a goal, then spends the next few nights visualising the dream holiday. She imagines the sights, sounds, textures, tastes and smells of the trip. She employs the First

Step Rule and goes online to research how much flights are, where they could stay, what the best areas are, how much a taxi from the airport would cost, and so on.

She works out that she'll need £5–7,000 for a trip like this, depending how much spending money they want to take. She looks at her finances and realises that, at the moment, there's not a clear path to how she would pay for it. She jots down a few ideas, e.g. putting it on a credit card, taking out a loan, seeing if she has any bonuses coming up at work, thinking about extra work she could do on the side. After writing her list, she decides to stay open-minded and wait for a flash of inspired action to take. She'd love for the holiday to manifest, but she's decided she's not going to stress out about it.

A few days later, in the shower, Person B remembers that she has a stack of old records in the garage that she's been meaning to put on eBay for ages. 'That could be a great start to a holiday savings fund!' she thinks. The next weekend, she takes out the records and starts searching online to find out how much they are worth. After selling the records, she's made over £500 towards the holiday, and it was super-simple. In fact, it was so easy that Person B has an idea to offer this as a service to neighbours and friends. She offers to list any items they have been meaning to sell for a while, with the agreement that she'll take a share of the profits. She has a few friends take her up on this offer and spends one day each weekend listing items.

Within a couple of months, Person B has made another

£1,000 towards her trip. One night, she comes across an online ad for a trip to another holiday destination. It's not where she had planned to take the family trip, but it actually looks pretty cool – in fact, it might be even better than the original destination she had in mind. What's more, they have an early-bird offer: if she puts down £1,500 now, she can pay off the rest at £500 a month until she travels. Person B uses her eBay money to put down the deposit and continues to run the listing service for friends and family, using the money to pay off the trip. They go on holiday and have a fabulous time.

There is nothing intrinsically right or wrong with either example. The first example shows someone who is attached to the outcome and will try to force it whatever happens. This has potentially led Person A to a somewhat less desirable outcome (more credit card debt) and nothing has been learned or gained to allow them to grow in the future.

For Person B, by contrast, not only has the process been less fraught and anxious, but our friend has also learned a new skill, which has opened up her mind to new ways of making money: a way that is fun and creative, and not how she would have previously thought about money coming to her. In being open-minded about how her goal could be reached, she was able to find an even better outcome than she would have expected, simply by being non-attached to how and when it happened.

It's not so much about the outcome being different: it's the process.

In Person B, we see someone who has taken inspired action – that's right, those little flashes of inspiration or 'shower ideas' should not be ignored! That's the magic! That is your subconscious brain throwing you a bone. We also see someone who is unattached to the process or the outcome. She knew she wanted to take a holiday, but she remained open-minded about how it might come about and didn't try to force the issue. Through this open-mindedness, she found new, creative ways of using her brain and remained open to money showing up in unexpected ways.

Person A has been more closed-minded. In her obsession with and attachment to the goal, her mind had already created the route she saw as being the only way to make the holiday happen. Who's to say that Person A doesn't also have a garage full of stuff to sell on eBay? The point is, in her attachment to the outcome and process, she was unable to spot opportunities to take inspired action. She was set in her ways, closed off to how it might happen, and therefore has not grown.

You might not think there is any problem with how Person A handles the situation. I mean, after all, they both ended up achieving their goal, right? And ultimately, we are reading this to achieve our money goals. Well, yes. But don't you see how Person B had a much more positive and enjoyable experience?

How did you feel, energetically, when reading Person A's experience? What was the vibe there? To me it felt frantic, controlling, busy, stressful and fraught. OK, the holiday at the end might have been amazing, but I wonder how she will feel coming back and having to pay off that trip for the next six months. Resentful, maybe? I don't know about you, but it didn't give me a warm, fuzzy feeling.

On the contrary, when I read Person B's experience, I am excited for her. The overall energy feels lighter, more opportunistic. I am happier for her reaching the goal in a surprising way and it feels good to know that she may have just stumbled across a potential new 'side hustle' to boost her income. Who's to say what the future of that might be? Overall, I find Person B's experience more fulfilling, lighter and calmer.

If you are unattached to the outcome, it will have no hold over you. You will not set expectations in your mind that could end up with you feeling let down or falling short. You will be more open-minded, and you will see more flashes of inspiration and ways to take inspired action. Your overall experience will be more enjoyable and undoubtedly more productive.

AVOIDING DESPERATION

Being attached to outcomes and the way in which things will happen is desperate. Desperation is one of the saddest emotions. It invokes pity and dismay rather than joy and positivity.

A lack of money can cause major desperation. I know

it. Some key decisions in my life and business have been made out of pure panic. But here's the question: does anything good ever come out of something created in those moments of panic?

In desperation, it's very hard for you to get a good result, because you're operating from a place of fear. Fear is not good for manifesting! When you feel desperate, it's hard to see the wood for the trees. You become so fixated on getting out of the dire circumstances you are in that you will take whatever option is thrown at you to move you on to the next step. Things that seem like a lifeline at the time can, in due course, turn out to have terrible consequences. You become accustomed to acting out of desperation and, in some sick twist, your desperation to get out of desperation creates a vicious circle.

Desperation has a frequency. It's quite low-vibe, right? You can just feel it in your bones, whether it's in yourself or in someone you encounter. Even just thinking about it makes my stomach drop. Not in an 'Ugh, gross' way, but in a way that recognises their despair and sadness. Some people really do find themselves in the most unfortunate situations and life can be most cruel. Sadly, this energy can be a turn-off for a lot of people – and some people will use it to exploit the desperate. Sensing that someone is in need doesn't always inspire people to part with their money, even though on paper it should. We should support those who need it, right? Well, in theory, yes, but I rarely see it play out that way.

It's like dating. You wouldn't keep texting someone to see if they want to go on a date with you if you've messaged once and they haven't replied. It would come off as desperate and unattractive.

At best, desperation will bring you pity money. At worst, it will bring you exploitation. Neither of these are high-vibe, nor will they be a positive force in helping you attract money. In order for you to start attracting money into your life, you have to know how to lift yourself out of desperation. So, how do we do that?

FIND THE GAP

The best way I have found to achieve non-attachment is to find the gap between thinking of a goal and trying to control the goal actually happening. It's a release, if you will. It reminds me of a quote from Don Draper in the TV show *Mad Men*: 'Just think about it, deeply, and then forget it. An idea will . . . jump up in your face.'

Don knew about the gap.

The gap is the moment before you start forcing your outcomes and expectations on to your new, fresh seed. It is where non-attachment happens. You set it, then forget it.

It's not that you don't care about if it happens or not, it's just that you aren't going to dwell on it. You're not going to obsess over it daily; at least, not in a negative way. You might spend time *thinking* about it daily, but not in a place of being desperate for it to happen. I always say, 'I want this to happen, but if for some reason or another it doesn't work out, that's OK, too.'

You might find this at odds with the work we did earlier around language and making sure to keep negative language out of our thoughts. But don't worry; saying that you are open to how the universe makes things happen for you isn't negative. It's trusting. You need to believe that whatever is meant to be will be: that if this thing that you want doesn't happen, there must be a good reason for it. Part of your life's work may be about working out what that reason is.

I recently came across this quote from Imam Al-Ghazali: 'What is destined will reach you, even if it be beneath two mountains. What is not destined will not reach you, even if it be between your two lips.'

Whether or not you believe in destiny, there is some comfort in believing that, if something is meant to happen for you, it will happen. This deep trusting or belief can be a huge relief to those of us who like to control every aspect of our lives. It might take some getting used to but, boy, is it a positive experience when you get there. It's a way of feeling that whatever happens, you're going to be all good. You'd be amazed at how freeing this can be. You might think this is living in airy-fairy dreamland, but sometimes you need to just zone out from the stresses of day-to-day worrying and start to be a bit more malleable. The openness and lightness this attitude provides will automatically help you lift your vibe, create a higher frequency and have a more positive outlook. That is sure to attract more greatness into your life.

It's all a self-fulfilling prophecy. Our beliefs can influence the outcomes. Believe that what is meant to be, will be, and, surprise, surprise: it all works out fine. You have changed your perception and filtered out the negative response you may once have had to your goal not turning out as you expected.

Applying the 'gap' to your goal setting

One area where we really try and enforce results is with our personal goals. As of now, I want you to try goal setting in a completely different way: a way where you are detached from the outcome – or 'in the gap'. It's about setting goals, but relinquishing control and expectations.

I find expectation to be a very hard thing to manage. Things often fall short of our expectations, so we can easily be left disappointed. By not setting an expectation around an idea or goal, we can free ourselves from all of the negative feelings that can go with it, such as pressure, worry and disappointment: feelings that are often experienced when we are trying to control the outcome of our goals. You never know – without much of an expectation, you could be pleasantly surprised with the results!

This goes against almost everything you've ever heard about goal setting, I know. After all, people in leadership roles often say that, when setting goals, we must have clear expectations. We are often trained to make our goals SMART (Specific, Measurable, Achievable, Realistic and Timely).

I'm not here to shit on SMART goal setting.

Goals *should* be specific and measurable. If they aren't, how do we know what we are trying to achieve, and how will we know when it's been achieved? Saying 'I want to look good' is vague and could be interpreted in many different ways. And how would you measure the success of this? Would it be when you feel that you look good? What if you feel that you look good one day and not the next? Is it when someone tells you? You can see why goals being specific and measurable is important, especially for the universe and your mind to be able to help you. But that's where my agreement with SMART goal setting ends.

Let's break it down.

'Achievable'? That's in the mind of the person setting the goal and, as we have seen, what a person believes is achievable is largely down to their conditioning. There is a whole world of what's achievable beyond what we might think. If we spend time only setting goals that we believe are 'achievable', we are cock-blocking ourselves. Do you think anyone would sit down with Elon Musk and tell him that his ideas aren't achievable?

Moving on to 'Realistic'. We all know that mad stuff can happen that is completely unexplainable or comes off as a miracle. Would you call this realistic? I think the word 'realistic' is code for LIMITED. And who is to say what's realistic?

By whose standards is it decided? If something is 'realistic' for us, does that mean it has to be based on what we, personally, have previously done? Worse still, does it have to be something that *others* consider 'realistic' for us? 'Realistic' is a trap, designed to keep you inside the containers of what you currently believe is logical.

And finally, 'Timely'. Well, that's about trying to control outcomes again, isn't it? I don't like to put time limits on things. It's another way of setting an expectation, and another way of being attached to how things pan out. What if you reach your goal one day after your set date: does that make it less of an achievement? Some things can manifest way sooner than you ever imagined. Sometimes, things can take years to show up. Who cares? We only care when we have an attachment to the outcome: usually, via desperation.

Ah, there we are – back to desperation. It's a plague that permeates almost everyone from time to time.

Alongside practising non-attachment, I found another nifty little trick to force myself out of times of desperation, and I want to share it with you.

DO THE ILLOGICAL

I remember sitting and staring at my laptop one day. I had my online banking on the screen, and my account had WAY less than I needed. It wasn't zero, but it wasn't looking too plump, if you know what I'm saying. I felt hopeless and angry at the world ... I had worked so hard and I had nothing to show for it. I noticed I was falling into victim mode and needed to snap out of it, sharpish.

How could I go from a victim's mentality to a champion's?

In that moment, it's like I had a little voice pop up inside my head (I now know to acknowledge things like this as moments of inspired action). The voice asked me, 'What's the thing that would be most in opposition to the obvious right now? What could bring about some good money karma?'

I sat and thought about it.

'Giving some money away.'

I almost gasped at myself.

Giving money away?!

It was in stark opposition to everything that felt right at that moment. 'Give money away, Sarah?! You don't have enough cash to pay your next four bills, but you want to give some money away? You are CRAZY!'

It seemed completely illogical.

But at the same time, part of me was intrigued. How could I quell this feeling of being broke? This sense of lack? By doing exactly what we wouldn't normally do in that situation. By being generous.

Why would adding fuel to the fire – in this case, me not having enough money and yet giving away some of what I did have – make any sense?

But the more I thought about it, the more it *did* make

sense. By being generous in my own time of need, I could not only break my own feelings of selfish victimhood, but also create a positive ripple in the world. If you believe in karma – and I do – it made sense that, at this very dark time, I could try to throw some light someone else's way. By doing so, I could start to feel better AND help others at the same time. It was the antidote to my negative feelings.

It also made sense on a 'real life' level. If I could give away money when I was at my lowest financial point and still be OK, maybe I was exaggerating the fear of the 'worst that could happen'. By being generous and giving, I could create a sense of abundance rather than lack.

So, I did it.

I went on to Facebook and scrolled through my news-feed until I found someone who was raising money on JustGiving. And I just went for it.

I donated £20.

OK, this might not be a life-changing amount, but at the time it felt like a LOT to me. And I don't know how or why, but I instantly felt better. The amount didn't matter: it was the act. An act of generosity doesn't need to be a mon-etary. You could give someone your time, for example, or share a skill.

It's now a rule of mine that, whenever I feel low or dark, I look for an action that seems to be the complete opposite of what my fear wants me to do. (In the example above, the 'logical' thing to do would be hoard money and cut all out-goings immediately.) This rule has never turned out badly for me, and has the almost instant effect of creating a feeling of lightness and non-attachment. I started off small, with little amounts, but now I find the bigger the gesture, the more I will be pulled out of my slump.

You can apply this 'doing the opposite' rule to any feeling. I often do it when I notice I am feeling jealous of a competitor. Instead of cutting ties or bad-mouthing them, I take opportunities to promote their work and praise them instead. It makes no sense, but it works. It takes you to a place of feel-good energy and humbles you at the same time.

LETTING GO

I bet it makes you feel weird to think about, it doesn't it?! Do you see how deeply ingrained into society our need to control everything is? I write this fully aware that I still have plenty of work to do in this area. I'm a big control freak and I still get caught on the idea of what's 'realistic', or on setting a goal and trying to force it to happen.

I realise, though, that this is a result of attachment being normalised. Remember that we are the odd ones out here. The world is still set up in a way that lacks belief in anything beyond the obvious or proven.

And remember: just because it can't be proven, doesn't mean it won't work.

€ *EXERCISE* €

Find the gap. Write a list of 25 things that you really, REALLY want. Be specific about exactly what those things are, but NOT how they'll happen. Cut out each thing and store the slips of paper in a jar. Pick one out to read out loud daily and add on 'and I am open to how and when it happens', at the end of each sentence.

CHAPTER 8

RICH IS A STATE OF MIND

Early on in my journey towards having a more positive money mindset, I would disclose my worries and fears at certain financial situations I had got myself into. Mine were fairly trivial: a late bill payment; birthday gifts I wanted to buy family members but couldn't; not being able to eat the things on the menu that I actually wanted; having people say, 'Oh hey, let's just split the bill,' after I had very carefully drunk two glasses of tap water and ordered a salad in order to keep my share down; or quite simply just seeing things that I wanted to own, but couldn't.

Feeling like you are not 'well off' or wealthy can be troubling on many levels. What if I said there was a way to release some of the weight of this, to alter your day-to-day state of mind and create a more peaceful vibe?

I learned early on that I needed to start channelling the rich person that I wanted to be in the future. And I needed to do it now. No, it wasn't about going out and dropping thousands on a car: I mean, I barely had single digits to drop on anything then, let alone thousands. It was about bringing forward the mindset of how someone who is wealthy would make decisions and day-to-day choices. How did they feel inside? Would they always settle, picking up the items in the grocery store that were on sale, or would they spend an extra 30p and get the organic strawberries that they actually wanted? I started to recognise the things I did, day to day, that made me feel wealthy, and the things that made me feel poor, or like I was settling for less.

In this chapter I'm going to train you how to 'act as if'.

'Acting as if' is a term often bandied about when we talk about manifesting and the Law of Attraction. The idea is to change your mindset and mentally embody the person you want to become in the future, today. Not necessarily physically, but in terms of how they would think and act. What would 'rich you' do about that bill that's due? What would 'rich you' think about the fee you're being offered on that project? What would 'rich you' do about that dream house you want to buy?

'Acting as if' is trying to bring forward how you believe the wealthy version of you will respond to situations in the future, and make your own response as close to that as possible in the current circumstances. It's very much a perception shift: changing your perception of yourself as someone who is broke and missing out to someone who has freedom of choice and the power that is associated with money. You've learned about how to control your perception already, and everything in this book so far has been leading you to this point. It's not about denying your current reality, it's about helping yourself realise that this is just the 'now' situation and that you can – and will – go beyond it, if you so wish.

The idea of acting as if can often be misconstrued. People see it as being the same as 'fake it till you make it', but it's totally different. 'Fake it till you make it' is just that – fake. Being fake with yourself and others will never bring about anything positive. It feels like a lie, a deception. Not only to others, but to yourself. How can you ever put yourself in the mindset of a rich person if you are using the terminology 'fake it till you make it'? Surely that would leave you feeling like a fraud and someone who is not worthy of money or opportunities: you have to 'fake it' to have them come your way. We are not trying to deceive anyone, least of all ourselves. With 'act as if' we are simply placing ourselves in the position of being able to take the same mental steps in decision-making that the future, wealthy you could.

HOW TO 'ACT AS IF' IN TIMES OF LACK

Let's say that you have just received a letter about an outstanding bill payment. Think of some words to describe how you might feel: stressed, chased, guilty, hounded, useless . . . these are just some that spring to mind when I think about it myself. Let's say you don't have the money to pay the bill right now, which is why it's late. Why does owing someone money feel so bloody awful?! Well, you should know by now that it's because you've been conditioned to feel that way.

Of course, if you owe someone money, you should aim to pay them on time. But let's be real for a second. These huge companies are used to late payments, yet, to you, it can feel like you are the only one with an outstanding payment. *You* are the one causing all the problems. *You* are the failure. This is the sort of downward thought spiral I used to go into. And do you know what often happens when we go into that spiral? We do one (or more) of the following.

- We bury our heads in the sand (*I'll just ignore that letter until I have the money or mental strength to deal with it*).
- We become defensive (*The world isn't fair. I work so hard and yet this shit still happens to me*).
- We become a victim (*I'm so sorry. I'm a useless human being; I can't believe I have put you through this*).

When you react in any of these ways, you have lost power and you have fallen into a negative, lack mindset.

Banks and businesses are built on this guilt-inducing stuff. I'm not saying you should ignore owing money to people or companies – of course not. But the world has been built on the notion of how powerful money is. Getting a late payment letter can feel like the company is saying: 'YOU OWE US MONEY AND IT'S THE END OF THE WORLD.' But can we just take a second to remember that almost the entire global economy is built on debt, borrowing, creating more money and bail-outs? If you look at it from afar, with your emotions detached, it's all just a bit of a game.

Banks, governments and corporations seem to be able to treat it like that, but to us, on a personal level, it can seem insurmountable. So, here's probably the most nonchalant thing I will say in this book:

Try not to let it bother you so much.

'Acting as if' is all about power. *Mental* power. Let's take the same situation and approach it with an 'act as if' mentality.

You get a letter about an outstanding bill payment. You open it and see the numbers in red that you owe.

Before you react, envision how future, wealthy you would react. Would she feel guilt, shame, panic, stress?

Let's walk through it. Firstly, future you would have the money in the bank to cover this right? (Don't worry if you don't right now. We are thinking of future you!) So, future you would have the money. Imagine it for a second. Close your eyes and imagine receiving the bill and reading the numbers but knowing that you have the money to cover it (and way more) in your account. You already feel lighter. There is no shame felt around the actual amount because you have it right there. You don't feel like a failure.

Why would there be a late bill payment if you had the money in the first place?

Simple. It's just an oversight! Future you has a lot of stuff going on: you might have your own business or be travelling a lot. Maybe you just moved house and they didn't have your correct address. Point is, it was an oversight. Again, close your eyes and imagine how the feeling around it being an oversight would be.

I think I would feel apologetic. I know that it's important to pay things on time out of courtesy, so I feel apologetic that I've missed the payment.

But I would not feel shame.

I would not feel guilt.

I would not beat myself up about it.

It is simply an oversight.

That feels way better, doesn't it? I don't feel like a victim. I feel like I have the power in my hands to make the situation right. It was just an oversight. It won't happen again!

Here's how future you would handle the situation.

- You would feel calm and collected about it.
- You would make an effort, straight away, to reach out to whoever had sent the bill. Explain the situation and handle it head-on.
- Rather than lingering on it, you would handle it and move on. (*Got more shit to do, I'm not dwelling on this! It's an insignificant part of my day.*)

Do you feel the difference in those two situations?

Now, I know you're probably thinking, 'But, Sarah, how does this actually change anything if I just don't have the money in my account to pay the bill?'

Well, what's happening in life at the moment does not need to be the reality you play in your mind. As you have seen from the chapter on visualisation, we can be quite good at creating new realities in our minds if we decide to.

What would change in this situation is your internal response. Instead of heading straight for 'I'm a shit person', go to 'I can handle this, it's just an oversight.' Reach out to the company or person who sent the letter STRAIGHT AWAY. Do not, I repeat DO NOT, bury your head in the sand and try to ignore the problem. Deal with it in a matter-of-fact way. If you don't have the money for it right now, that's OK. You know why? Because this situation is TEMPORARY.

Repeat after me ...

This is temporary.

Call the company. Explain there has been an oversight and you aim to bring your account into alignment as soon as possible. Ask what they can do to help make this payment more manageable for you. Perhaps you can't pay it all in one go right now, but you can pay an agreed amount today, then clear the rest on an agreed date. You will be surprised at how flexible and accommodating people can be when you actually just HANDLE YOUR SHIT.

Ignoring problems and hoping they will go away is child-ish, and it's the trait of a person with a lack mentality. You are not that. Pick up the phone. Make the call. Someone with an abundant mindset isn't afraid to handle their shit because, even if they are having a challenging moment right now, they know that the situation is temporary, and light is around the corner. Go into it with that mentality.

In the second version of events, you retain power. Instead of giving your power away, along with your dignity, you have kept both. You have handled the situation honestly and in an adult manner.

This is not 'faking it'. This is *owning it*.

You are owning that this is a temporary situation and that you will soon be moving past this challenging area. 'Acting as if' is not about spending money and faking a lifestyle. It's not even about money at all. It's about mindset.

WHAT IS REALLY HAPPENING WHEN WE 'ACT AS IF'?

There are a few reasons I believe 'acting as if' works that I want to share with you.

When we 'act as if', we are helping to bring what we want to happen closer to us. Playing the 'one day' game is easy, but what if that one day was now? Your environment may not reflect the wealth you will have in the future, but your mind can go to a place that can experience how it might feel emotionally. Any taste of the future that you can give yourself now, in the present moment, is incredibly important in helping your subconscious believe that you are a person who can have it, who is worth it and who deserves it.

You are allowing yourself to experience the freedom that comes along with wealth. Before now, you had been denying yourself that freedom because you had fallen victim to the feelings we have been conditioned to have about money: guilt, shame, denial ... I could go on.

Eleanor Roosevelt said, 'No one can make you feel inferior without your consent.' Well, no one should be able to make you feel broke without your consent, either.

Not having enough money in this exact moment does not mean that you are an inferior person. Keep in mind the mentality a rich person would have and don't listen to the inner voice that says 'you're a shitty person' just because you don't have much in your account.

You can start to experience the mindset of a rich person, right here and right now. Mentally creating the image of yourself being wealthy helps with any feelings you may have around worthiness. I know a lot of people can struggle with picturing themselves as someone who could ever have money, but as you work on it, just as you read in the visualisation chapter, you can make that mental picture clearer and clearer. Seeing yourself as and 'acting as if' you are the person you aspire to become can create huge jumps in your own personal worth. No one is more or less deserving of money. It is a game to be played and won.

On a magical level, when you act as if you have the money and freedom of mind you want, it sends some kind of energy forcefield out around you. The way people see you changes, probably because you are carrying yourself with more value and worth. As soon as you start taking yourself seriously and start placing higher value on yourself, the universe recognises that.

A great example of this is pricing your own services. In my online education business, No Bull Business School, we have a lot of students who are freelance or have their own businesses. Pricing their own products and services often comes up as an area that people struggle with, continually undervaluing themselves due to feelings of inferiority or lack of worth. 'What would a rich person do in this situation?' I ask them, when news of them accepting a shabbily low rate for effort-heavy work reaches me. 'Would a rich person accept that rate? Or would they value themselves more highly? And would they feel worried in any way about going back to the client to quote a higher rate? No. Because they know they are worth it.' I've seen numerous students start to value themselves more highly and channel the 'act as if' mentality, then go back to their client and negotiate a rate that they are excited about receiving.

When you show the universe or the world around you that you take yourself seriously, other people will take you seriously too. This doesn't need to wait until you have a certain amount of money in your account. It's not 'when I get X, I will feel like this'. Instead, it's 'when I feel like this, I will get X'.

That's the part you *really* need to get your head around.

'ACTING AS IF' MAKES SHIT HAPPEN QUICKLY

You know the saying 'It's better to have loved and lost than never to have loved at all'? I believe the opposite to be true with money. I think it would probably be even more painful to have had a lot of money, then lost it, than never to have known the freedom that money can bring. I know that sounds ridiculous – after all, look at the incredible suffering we have in the world – but because so much of the world's issues focus around money, to have had it and then lost it, or had it taken away from you must be quite traumatising.

Do you have a resistance to that statement? Even as I wrote it, I could feel my own resistance: 'Ooh, poor rich person, losing their money!' But try to think about it without judgement. You might think the person in question was bloody lucky to have had even a taste of the good life at all. But imagine tasting it and then having it taken away, never to be experienced again. That would be painful.

The reason I mention it is because it's also part of why 'acting as if' is so powerful. Once you've had a taste of what it could be like, you won't want it to disappear. You will want it to happen again, and again, or be something you can experience regularly. Feeling, touching and tasting the things you want in life can help you make them a reality faster. So 'acting as if' can actually help to speed up your journey by boosting your motivation.

If you can try in any way to experience the life you want now, DO IT.

Before I started doing any work on my money mindset, if I had taken a flight and was asked to walk through first class to get to my economy seat, I would have felt like it was an utter piss-take.

'Of course, they're making us poor people walk through first class to get to our shit seats! Look at them, rubbing their wealth in our faces. Who would pay six grand for a plane ride anyway?' I would have said.

Recently, when we went on a family holiday to LA, we had to walk through first class. Having done a lot of money mindset work, I decided to use this opportunity to plant some manifesting seeds in my brain. As we walked through first class, I made sure to walk very slowly. I looked around and took in all of the details. The stitching on the leather, the spacious seats, the colour of the wood grain. I ran my hands along the back of each seat as I walked past. I felt the luxurious, soft blanket that was on one of the seats. I took in the quietness of the space. I did all of this on purpose, to make myself even more frustrated with my economy seat!

'Why would you want to make yourself frustrated, Sarah?' you might ask.

Well, I wanted to experience what it would be like to have the luxury of being able to fly first class. Instead of being judgemental and spending time projecting my own money judgements on to those who could afford it, I looked at it with joy and a sense of wonder, thinking, 'Wow, how lovely it must be to fly first class!'

When I got to my economy seat, I focused on the frustration of having to cram into my little chair. Now this is the point where you might wonder why I am not banging on about gratitude. I have a weird relationship with gratitude. A lot of writing on the Law of Attraction can be pretty heavy-handed about it: Be grateful for your job! Be grateful for your shit boss! Be grateful that you are cleaning a toilet today!

Gratitude is important, of course, especially when it comes about organically. But I don't think you should spend time being 'fake grateful' for things that you want to change. Frustration is a powerful action, and one that I find positive. It's not about moaning for no reason; it's about saying, 'I want to change this for the better' and finding ways to do so. The frustration of wanting to upgrade your lifestyle can power you forward. My feeling that day was: 'I'm so happy that we can take an amazing family holiday to LA. And next time, I'll make sure we can fly first class!' You can acknowledge the positives of a situation without denying that, yeah, you still want better. AND THAT'S OK.

I also find that when I am 'acting as if' or even 'thinking as if', it helps me to realise that certain things I want in life aren't as far away as I have always considered them to be.

When I started working on my money mindset, I joined a gym. It was a very basic gym, with one of those £18-a-month subscriptions. I had suffered with stress and anxiety and wanted to see if exercise could help me to overcome these a little bit. I had also looked at all of the successful entrepreneurs I admired, and I realised that all of them had made exercise a priority in their lives. So, I 'acted as if' and I got myself a gym membership. I was doing some basic workouts, but I was really struggling to motivate myself and found that I had all but stopped going. I didn't really understand how to use the machines, I had no accountability, I didn't know which parts of my body I should be trying to work on and I didn't know what combination of exercises to do. I was a total newbie! I kept saying to myself, 'If only I had a personal trainer.' That way, I'd be held accountable, I'd have someone to help me reach my goals and I'd feel less anxious about using some of the intimidating gym equipment. Having a personal trainer seemed like something only rich people did, though. After all, it was so expensive! Or was it? I actually had no idea how much a personal trainer cost. I'd never even looked into it because I'd told myself it was something I would be able to afford 'one day' but definitely not now.

You can guess what I did next, right? I followed the First Step Rule.

First, I researched how much using one of the gym's personal trainers would cost. When I looked into it, I was surprised to find that they gave you a free taster session to try it out. 'Act as if,' I thought. Even if I couldn't afford to do any sessions beyond the first one, I knew that the act of taking the taster session would put me into the headspace of someone who had a personal trainer. If nothing else, I'd learn a few exercises and perhaps feel more confident using the gym equipment. But I'd also be a step closer to feeling like someone who could have a personal trainer. It would help me visualise it and 'act as if' better in the future. So, I took the taster session.

It was actually super fun and I learned loads, for free. There wasn't even a sales pitch at the end of the session, so I didn't need to do an awkward 'back away' from something I couldn't afford.

(Pop quiz! What language could you use instead of 'can't afford'? Let's say it was 'a little outside of my allocated budget' at that time.)

After I had the session, it felt so much easier to visualise having weekly sessions with a personal trainer. It had made the possibility feel so much more real, and I wanted it so much more! I felt the burn in my muscles the following day and I could see how, if I did this consistently, it could really make a difference to my body and mind.

I came to the decision that I was going to make getting a personal trainer a priority, and so I spoke to the guy who had trained me at the gym. I asked him if there was any wiggle room on pricing or sessions. Could I do a deal and trade some of my expertise for his time? Maybe I could help him grow his Instagram account or create better videos? To my surprise, the cost of the sessions was a lot more reasonable than I first thought. And what's more, he mentioned that he would be happy to offer thirty-minute sessions at half the price of a usual hour-long session. Thirty minutes each week was still plenty of time to feel the burn! Because I could see how valuable and productive this would be for me both physically and mentally, I decided to go for it.

I stopped spending in other areas, cutting back on takeaways and junk food, and instead I put that money back into my training. Four years later, exercise has become an integral part of my life, and it's done me the world of good! I'm annoyed at myself that I didn't discover the power of exercise until I was thirty years old, but that's another story.

LET'S ANALYSE WHAT HAPPENED HERE AND HOW IT WORKED

I envisioned what a rich version of me would be doing: in this case, having a personal trainer.

Instead of saying, 'Oh, that'll never happen,' or setting it aside for 'one day', I decided to 'act as if', in that moment.

I took the free taster session to get a real-life feeling of what it would be like to have a personal trainer.

The free taster session helped me get into the mind-set of someone with a personal trainer. I could 'act as if' and visualise even better!

Because I could feel how it would be to have a trainer, I started to make it a priority in my life. Having experienced it, I knew I really wanted it.

I followed the First Step Rule and I did the research to find out the actual costs rather than making an assumption.

Instead of hiding away from the amount, I faced it head-on and spoke to the trainer about a deal we could work out.

The point of sharing this story is that we often tell ourselves things are further beyond our reach than they actually are. We tell ourselves they are too expensive, too time-consuming, not for us, etc. These are mental blocks, and you are putting them up yourself – probably to keep you inside your comfort zone. I get it, it's nice there! It's cosy and warm and no one is challenging you. Sounds pretty sweet, right? Sure, comfort zones are nice and it's good to spend some time there. But not ALL of your time. Because there is no progress inside your comfort zone.

Every time you step outside your comfort zone, you make it a bit bigger. It's like stepping from your soft, cosy space into the cold outside and laying down some rugs and cushions and warm blankets. If you don't step outside the borderline, it'll never grow. Wouldn't you like an even bigger cosy space? 'Acting as if' is a great way to enlarge your comfort zone and bring into your current reality the person you want to be in the future. Follow the First Step Rule and then 'act as if', and find a way to experience something at an affordable price that gives you that feeling of wealth. We all know that, the more we feel that feeling, the more of those good-vibe feelings we will 'attract'. Spending a little and not settling for less than what you'd like might seem detrimental as it does cost money, but the feeling it gives you – and what that feeling creates – is worth its weight in gold!

Anything is possible. Don't take what's on paper as the final answer. You can always negotiate, ask for deals, trade services, barter on price and more. What would 'rich you' do? Would she take the going rate? Nah, mate! She would know she has the power to negotiate and get a great deal. Don't you always find that people with money are the first ones to try and get a good deal? They know the value of their cash and they are willing to stand up for themselves and get really good value for money.

Just because you don't have a million in your account doesn't mean that you can't hold the mental power to strike a great deal or get value for money. Believe you have just as much negotiating power as a millionaire and watch what happens.

MAKING THINGS A PRIORITY

I couldn't go through this chapter without touching on priority. We often dwell on things we haven't managed to manifest, but if you take a step back and ask yourself honestly, 'Did I make this a priority?' the answer is likely to be no.

Unless you make something a priority, it's unlikely to happen. And, trust me, it's hard if you have too many priorities going at once. Especially when it comes to things you are trying to do around money. At first, it helps to focus on one thing at a time that you're trying to make happen. Get in touch with why it's so important to you. What would it change in your life? How would your day to day be better?

I once read a book called *The One Thing* by Gary Keller, which explained that the key to success was doing one thing at a time. This can be applied to money and manifesting the things you want. In *The One Thing*, Keller wrote that, if you do one thing well, you have to be ready for other things to mound up around you while you focus on it. I've seen that to be true. As you focus so much on one area, life can build up around you as you don't have the time or mental space to give it thought. You have to be OK with this and get used to it.

As mentioned in Chapter 6, I've had a trip to Japan on my vision board for many years now. Has it happened yet? No – because I haven't been making it a priority. I've put most of my focus into growing my online education business, No Bull Business School, and that is the area where I see all of my manifesting paying off. I have no doubt that, if I decided tomorrow to make going to Japan a priority, it could happen sooner.

WHAT WOULD YOU LIKE TO BE YOUR NEW MONEY PRIORITIES?

It could be paying off a debt, getting paid a better salary, going on holiday, putting down a deposit on a house . . . it's up to you. Just make sure it is a priority.

List your top three new money priorities below:

1.
2.
3.

SOME QUICK 'ACT AS IF' HACKS

Power poses

If you have never heard of power poses, these are physical poses that you can assume which lead to you feeling more powerful, relaxed and in control. Power poses in themselves are a version of 'acting as if'.

Power poses will vary from person to person, depending on what you see as being strong and powerful. For many people, this could be a hands-on-hips pose, almost like Wonder Woman. It's not so much about the pose itself, but what it brings to mind. A strong woman who won't take any shit! Or it could be leaning back in a chair with your feet on the desk and your arms behind your head. That reminds me of a cocky man who doesn't give a damn. Maybe the pose is standing and leaning forward on to a desk with your hands spread. That position has urgency and strength. None of these power poses actually *makes* you more powerful, but they can help you to *feel* more powerful.

You know the drill: when you walk taller and hold your head higher, it does make you feel like you can handle your shit. Next time you're worrying about money, think about how the future 'rich you' would hold herself, and adopt that pose. It might help you to quickly change your mood!

Try it on

I would always feel that going into designer stores was something I'd only be able to do once I'd made a certain amount of money, as if they scan your bank balance upon entry or something. I made myself feel like I wasn't good enough to touch the clothes or even enter the shop. But I thought back to the quote, 'No one can make you feel inferior without your consent'.

So, I started pushing myself to go into designer stores, and touch and hold the luxury items. I would try on the dresses, feel the fabrics, talk to the staff as if I deserved to be there. Because I did! I never actually spent any money. But by going in and feeling as if I was allowed to be there, it made me feel more like it could be a possibility. It also brought it all so much closer to home.

Turns out, the staff are always AMAZING in these places and will often fuss over you and treat you brilliantly. Never once did I have a *Pretty Woman* moment and get pushed out of the shop.

Think of a place that you find scary to enter because you don't feel like you deserve to be there. It could be a fancy hotel, a designer store, a cosmetics store, a gym. You don't need to actually spend any money! Find out what free tasters you can get, or simply try on the clothes. YOU ARE ALLOWED TO DO THAT! Get a real-life experience of what living that feels like, then use it to fuel your goals.

Ask yourself

Whenever faced with a decision, ask yourself: 'How would a rich person handle this?' Remember, it's not always about spending money. It's about mindset and finding your inner power.

¥ *EXERCISE* ¥

Download and listen to the 'future you' audio guide at www.themoneyiscoming.com this week before bed. Step into knowing what is coming to you. From now on, 'act as if'.

£

CHAPTER 9

SAY NO TO SAY YES!

There are a lot of personal challenges in this book, and you will probably feel some resistance to what I'm asking you to do because it will push you outside of your comfort zone. As Jen always said to me, 'If you want to change your life, you need to change your life.'

Of course, you will encounter resistance; it's normal. I've been building you up bit by bit, starting with the easy stuff – you know, questioning how the world works, how you think, and helping you to make small, internal adjustments. You have probably found them fun and quite easy to implement.

You will, no doubt, find these final two chapters the most challenging. While you are in this transition phase of trying to do a complete one-eighty, going from feeling negative about money to feeling positive about money, you'll need to put yourself first. That might mean that a few people get put out about it – you need to be OK with that.

It may feel like we have whizzed through this money-manifesting journey, but you should already be seeing some monumental changes in how you think and behave when it comes to money. As we approach the end of the book, I couldn't finish without spending a bit of time talking to you about worth.

'Know your worth' seems to be a popular catchphrase of the moment. It's perfect social media fodder (in fact, I'm sure I've personally posted it as a quote somewhere, so, guilty as charged!). But what exactly does it mean to know your worth? And how can you know your worth when, for so long, you've been feeling completely and utterly CRUD about money?

It's all well and good to shout, 'Yasss babes, know your worth!' at your fellow sisters, but it loses its impact when you don't apply it to yourself. Many of us think that we have to accept any work/money/attention that comes our way. And I do really mean ANY. It's what we've been taught, right? Beggars can't be choosers and all that. But I'd beg to differ. Beggars *can* be choosers. In fact, it's really bloody important that you are a chooser. Being a chooser has nothing to do with being entitled or too big for your boots: it's a damn necessity.

CLOSE ONE DOOR, THEN OPEN ANOTHER

Throughout my years of working with women, I have learned that we are often very, very afraid of saying no. Of the thousands of women I have interacted with, I'd say only a handful have been able to say no to people and their requests without then agonising over it for hours, days and weeks afterwards, wondering what people will think of them for having said it. We might want to say no to something that doesn't fit us, doesn't suit our lifestyle, isn't what we want to do, or – crucially – something that pays less money than we want to accept. All too often, we end up saying yes to it, then hate the result because we didn't want to do it in the first place. So why should we feel bad for saying no?

Because we've been taught to 'play nice'.

Putting yourself first and going for what you want is not seen as a 'nice' trait for people to have. We're taught to be kind and selfless and to always put everyone else first. I'm not saying don't ever do that: I'm just saying there are moments when you are *allowed* to put yourself first – and where you should. In fact, it's incredibly healthy.

This fear of saying no is crippling. It will hold you back from trying to attract more money. It's the kryptonite to wealth and it will keep you in the same spot for years on end with no progress. I'm sorry to be blunt, but it's true.

Be kind, be honest, help people? Yes. But don't bend over backwards for everyone else so far that what *you* want gets lost in the sauce. Life is short. Don't get to your deathbed and realise that, while helping everyone else get ahead, you stayed in exactly the same position. I know you don't want that, or you wouldn't have picked this book up.

Please hear me when I say this:

We have to get OK with saying no.

When something comes your way, be it an opportunity, an offer of work or a potential collaboration, your reaction needs to be either a 'hell yeah' or a 'hell NO'. Life is too short to waste time on things that don't make you happy, or things you are doing because you feel you ought to.

Let's say you are a graphic designer. You have just gone freelance and you want to start building your portfolio. It's been slow-going as you're brand new to the industry and don't have a huge body of work to prove your expertise just yet. One day, a friend puts you in touch with an acquaintance of hers who wants some graphic design work done. The work isn't anything you'd be excited about doing, but you think, 'At least it's a job.'

When you speak to this potential client, you're not filled with any kind of enthusiasm. In fact, the client seems like he could be really hard work going forward. Something about the way he talks to you makes you feel a little bit patronised and you can't put your finger on it, but your gut feeling is that you won't enjoy working him.

You decide to ignore your gut. The logical side of your brain kicks in. You want to get your freelance work off the ground, and who are you to be choosy at this point anyway?

Your friend tells you it might not be the perfect job, but at least it's something to get you started.

When the work comes through, it's a larger project than you expected and quite time-consuming. You need to go back to your client with a quote. It's your first job and you want to secure the work. Those bills aren't gonna pay themselves! Also, just having something on paper to show future clients would surely be helpful, even if it's not really the kind of thing you want to be working on. You come up with a fee that's less than what you'd usually charge, then reduce it down even further. 'That seems fair,' you think. You agonise over the pricing for ages, thinking you're probably still quoting too much, and end up reducing the quote still further. You finally send the email.

A few days go by, and you worry and worry about the fact that you've probably quoted too high a fee. You're worrying yourself sick – maybe this freelance life isn't for you after all. How do people do this? It's agonising!

Days later, you finally get a reply. The client is not happy with the pricing and asks if you can bring it in line with his budget. He remarks, 'I could get someone else to do it for less, but Sophie said you needed the work, so I thought you could do me a good deal.' You feel put out, patronised and low, but you need the work. You agree to his offer.

You start working on the project and the next few weeks are hell. Working with this client is a nightmare – your gut was totally right about him being a pain in the ass. 'Why did I agree to this?! I KNEW it would be a nightmare!' you think.

Every time you get out your laptop to work on his project (which he chases you about non-stop, without giving you proper time to work on it), you feel a strong pang of resentment and anger towards the client.

As you finally hand the last bit of work in, you reflect on what happened. Not only was it an unenjoyable experience, but you're not even proud of the work you did. He insisted on so many tweaks and changes that it's not something you'd ever put in your portfolio anyway. So, what was it all for? To top it all off, he is over a month late paying you, which means you miss a payment for a bill and get a fine.

GAHHHHH!

This is toxic. By accepting this work, the graphic designer in this example was putting it out there – to the universe, to her subconscious, to who knows – that she wasn't good enough to wait for a client who valued her. She was desperate and took the first thing that came along.

Did you find yourself nodding along to this? Has it happened to you? Almost everyone I know who has worked for themselves at any point has experienced almost exactly this scenario. In fact, it can happen to anyone, whether you own your own business or not. How often do you find yourself saying yes to doing a favour for someone who never returns it? Or taking on a project at work that you really don't wanna do? Or accepting a job offer because it pays better but is less fulfilling?

Would a rich person do those things? Nope. Because they know they don't need to.

I know this part is hard, because we can all find ourselves in very desperate situations. Trust me, I know. But letting desperation lead you into accepting stuff that is not in line with what you want is troublesome. Also, let's just talk about the major mistake our graphic designer friend made ... she ignored her gut.

Your gut instinct will not fail you. That feeling that something is 'off', or a sense that you're likely to resent something about this situation further down the line is your gut trying to guide you to a decision that is right for you. It feels bad when someone says, 'I told you so.' But do you know what feels way worse? When your own brain is like, 'SARAH, I TOLD YOU WEEKS AGO ABOUT THIS! WHY DIDN'T YOU LISTEN TO ME? I EVEN THREW OUT SOME HORMONES THAT MADE YOU FEEL SICK AND LIKE YOU MIGHT SHIT YOURSELF AND YOU STILL DIDN'T LISTEN TO ME! WHAT WILL IT TAKE?'

Yeah, that feels awful. Because you know you could have done something about it, but you didn't.

Alongside not listening to her gut, our graphic designer also made a conscious decision to agree to create work that wasn't in line with the type of customer she wanted to attract. The Law of Attraction works across the board, not just around money. If what she'd actually love to do is create really cool, girly, streetwear-inspired graphic design, and she's accepting work from someone who wants a boring corporate slideshow, is that in line with her aspirations? Nope. So not only is she subconsciously telling herself she's not good enough to get the jobs she wants, she is unlikely to ever actually get those jobs because the work she's done is in the wrong style. If I'm looking for a graphic designer to do my cool, girly, streetwear-style website, I'm not going to pick the person who has a portfolio full of navy blue and grey corporate design jobs. I'll pick the person who has examples of exactly what I want.

You see how it works?

Be clear about what you want and put it out there. Create it. Act as if. Then watch it come.

The most troubling problem with the kind of interaction in our example above is that it all just leaves you feeling low-vibe. It makes you feel lesser-than. Unworthy. There is absolutely nothing empowering about this kind of interaction. It creates resentment and, let me tell you, resentment will eat at you day and night. It will breed negativity and create stress. It needs to be cut out, like a cancer.

I have seen people accept situations like this over and over and over again. You might think, 'Why? Why on earth would you take such a load of shit from someone you owe nothing to?'

But it's so easy to say that about someone else's situation; it's much harder to handle it yourself. We often don't value ourselves highly enough and will discount our skills, talents and value in order to make someone else comfortable.

Enough is enough. You must learn to say no. Say no to a basic project offer because you know you're destined for something more challenging. Turning away a crap client allows space for a great client to walk in. You must believe this. It will keep you sane and stop you accepting rubbish that doesn't serve you.

A 'no' doesn't need to be rude. You can say it quite politely. You can softly decline a request. You can even make some shit up to get out of anything you don't want to do. Obviously it is best to be honest if you can: it will build your confidence and future ability to say no. In a worst-case scenario, though, if you really need to and it makes the difference between you actually feeling able to say no or not, just make something up. Don't accept anything that makes you feel less than what you know your worth to be.

Saying no to people can be hard. You'll often be met with shock, even attitude on occasion. Hearing a 'no', especially from a woman who stands in her 'no' proudly and strongly, can be shocking to some people.

Let me just tell you this.

You are always entitled to say no.

You do not owe anyone an explanation as to why you have said no.

You never need to justify a 'no'.

You never need to feel bad about a 'no'. Give yourself a break. You know your reasons.

No one can make you feel bad about a 'no'. They can try, but you must resist.

You must never agonise over a 'no'. You must say it and move on. If other people want to sit down and dissect your 'no', that's on them.

A 'NO' HELPS EVERYONE GET WHAT THEY WANT

Often people worry about saying no because they think it will let someone down. The truth is, it actually does the opposite.

If you say no to someone, you are allowing that person to find the right fit for them. Because you are not the right fit. Our friend who accepted the graphic design job was not the right fit for the project. Not only did it lead to her feeling low and unworthy, no doubt the client was getting frustrated, too. He didn't have a designer on board who felt passionate about the project. He had someone who felt resentful and undervalued. As a result, she probably wouldn't have been putting in as much effort to the work, meaning the situation wasn't fair on the client, either.

The thing with these types of interactions is that we can 'feel' the energy. Sometimes stuff just feels 'off'. You don't vibe with someone for whatever reason, or you can almost feel someone's pent-up resentment when you speak to them. I don't have any scientific reason as to why exactly this happens: sometimes things just *feel weird*.

On the contrary, if our graphic designer had declined the work and the client had kept looking for someone else, maybe he would have found the perfect designer for his project: someone who was just as excited about his corporate slideshow as he was. They could have had a very happy working relationship for many months.

If you accept opportunities, clients, jobs, requests, etc.,

that you know in your gut aren't right for you, you are actually doing a disservice to the person you are 'helping'. You might think, 'Yeah but that client was low-balling her, so he deserves shit service.' Well, he's not necessarily being completely evil here. Perhaps he's a little naïve, but I don't think it would have been the client's intention to deliberately make her feel undervalued. This leads me to my next point.

YOUR WORTH IS NOT DETERMINED BY OTHERS: IT'S DETERMINED BY YOU

What people offer you, money-wise, is nothing to do with you. It's about them.

The client in the example above offered our designer friend less than her worth. Was that anything to do with her? Nope. It was to do with *his* perceived value of what she did and how it would affect him. It's all about how her work fitted into his map of the world and he placed a monetary value on it accordingly. Maybe the project wasn't that important to him. Maybe someone had done similar work for him more cheaply before, so that's where his marker was. I repeat. NONE OF IT WAS TO DO WITH HER ACTUAL WORTH.

You can never go at people with attitude because of how much they are offering you in payment. People will have their own perceived value of things – of you, even. Your knowledge of your own worth has nothing to do with what other people are willing to pay. It's up to you to know what you are willing to accept.

I see people get angry about this often. 'Can you believe they only offered to pay me X for that job?! Fuckers!' In my opinion, this anger is misplaced. It puts someone else at fault for not being able to see *your* worth. Seeing your worth is not the job of other people. You dictate your worth, and it is your job to help people to see it. If they can't, for whatever reason, that's OK. You can smile and move on. Sitting and stewing over why someone isn't willing to pay you what you're worth is going to bring your vibe down. It also feeds into a victim mentality and, as you know by now, you're not a victim at all. *You* control what's going on in your life, not anyone else.

When people place too low a value on me and what I do, I am more than happy to say no and move along. Should they question it, I'm also more than happy to explain to someone why I am worth more. And that comes from having an inner confidence about who I am as a person and the value that I bring to people. Right now, you may not feel that you have that inner confidence. It's easy not to have it, especially when you have been concerned about your cash flow. Society puts high value on people with money, success and power, and it can be easy to feel like you are at the bottom of the food chain when you haven't been having a great time financially.

But I'll let you in on a secret. Your worth and confidence

will not increase once you have more money. It's the other way around.

You will have more money when your worth and confidence increase.

You need to do the inner work first.

HOW TO LOVE YOURSELF

You are fucking amazing, and sometimes you can be the last bloody person to see it. When I say to 'love yourself', I don't mean you need to be out there showing off and banging on about how you're the greatest person on the planet. I mean you need to respect yourself and be able to see your own greatness. Let me help you out.

Do you want to love yourself?

If your answer is yes, great! If your answer is no, it's worth looking at what is going on underneath the surface, because it may be more than I'm able to advise on. If you struggle with answering that question, I would suggest looking at seeking some professional help from a counsellor who could help you work through what's happening. And please do! Because I can tell, you're pretty awesome – I mean, you bought my book! So, do what you need to do in order to be able to stomach the idea of loving yourself. Because it's an absolute must.

Let go of comparison

Comparison is a big problem, especially since social media showed up. Everyone has good bits and bad bits. You need to work out what makes you YOU and really embrace those attributes. OK, Sally might have perfect hair, but does she have your quick maths skills? Can she be the cool aunt that all your nieces and nephews love? We all have our thing. Get honest about what your thing is. For instance, I will never be elegant. I have an awkward figure that's bony and runs straight up and down. I hunch over and I walk like a teenage boy. But I'm fucking smart. I can learn technology fast. I can do a mean cat-eye flick with my eyeliner. It's not about comparing what you can't do with what someone else can do. It's about looking at all the things that make you great and enjoying those aspects of yourself.

Go all in on what makes you YOU

We are often conditioned to think that investing in what we love, whether that's a hobby, your sneaker collection or an evening painting class can be frivolous: a bad use of money or time. But listen: it's not. Go where feels good. Do whatever makes you feel great. If you have a passion for something and you want to spend your money on it, DO IT. If it feels high-vibe to you, go for it. I'm not saying get into debt over these things. I'm not saying you should spend the £50 you owe to the electricity company on some new make-up. I'm saying when you have the chance to 'treat yourself', please do it without guilt. Because investing in the things you love is a sure-fire way to increase your self-worth and raise your vibes.

> ## WRITE DOWN FIVE THINGS THAT MAKE YOU AWESOME. ANYTHING GOES!
>
> 1.
> 2.
> 3.
> 4.
> 5.

A FEW TIPS ON SAYING NO

If I haven't quite drummed it in yet, YOU NEED TO GET BETTER AT SAYING NO. This can be quite a challenge for people, so I thought I'd share a few tips on some wording you can use to politely decline things that don't align with you.

Try this:

'Thank you so much for your offer. As much as I'd like to help . . .'

' . . . I am focused on different goals right now.'

' . . . I don't think I'm going to be the right person for the job, but I have a recommendation for you.'

' . . . You deserve someone who can give this their full attention and I'm not sure I can do that for you right now.'

' . . . I have some big goals I'm trying to achieve at the moment and I really need to focus my energy there.'

Now, all of this talk of knowing your worth and saying no is great, and it'll save you a lot of aggro and headspace. But there is something bigger at play here.

SOMETHING BETTER IS COMING

There are many reasons I want you to say no to things. It will keep your day-to-day stress levels lower, it will help you enjoy your day more, it will stop you from feeling resentful. But the most important thing to know is that, when you say no to something, you are sending a signal.

You're signalling to the universe that you value yourself enough to wait for the thing that is *right*. You are not afraid of doors closing on old chapters of your life. Old, broke chapters! You are saying goodbye to your old life and welcoming in a new, abundant, rich life. In order to do that, you need to cut the crap and say goodbye to shit that doesn't work for you. You deserve better, you *know* you deserve better, and you're willing to say no to the stuff that doesn't fit with where your life is going. You are waiting for things to show up that are aligned with your goals: things that make you feel valued, respected, rich and high-vibe.

You are saying that you know, trust and believe that something better is on its way for you. That you are ready for it, so that when this thing that is bigger and better shows up for you, you will take inspired action and grab it with both hands.

Because *this* is what you have been waiting for.

☙ *EXERCISE* ☙

Make a list of things that you have said yes to in the past that have left you feeling resentful or undervalued. It could include favours for friends or family, work commitments, projects, etc. We're not going to sit and dwell on them. Instead, write down the key lessons that you took from each one. What was your gut saying that you didn't listen to? What did you learn about yourself that you can take forward to make sure you don't end up in a similar position again?

Use the 'Should I say no?' checklist below to start saying NO.

Ask yourself these questions:

- Is this something I am genuinely excited about?
- Will this help me to move towards my goals?
- Would I do this if I had a good amount of money in my account?
- Will this leave me feeling 'high-vibe'?
- Does this project or opportunity align with who I am and the things I am interested in?

Use your answers to these questions to determine whether this is something worth your time. If not, say no and move on. Do not let yourself agonise over it. Remember: you are also doing the other person a disservice if you accept without the right intentions. Get used to saying no.

You can also head to www.themoneyiscoming.com and download the PDF worksheet for this chapter.

$

CHAPTER 10

YOUR NEW LIFE IS GOING TO COST YOU YOUR OLD ONE

You know there is likely to be some resistance to change. It's entirely normal, so don't feel freaked out or think you're useless if you find yourself going back to your old negative language or feelings around money.

You may want to come back to this book over and over again; I'd be so happy if it found a place in your home so that you can refer back to it whenever you need to. My dream is for you to highlight sections and underline bits and thumb through it so many times the pages fall out of the spine.

While you're in the process of change, it can still be triggering to see others enjoy their wealth when you sometimes still feel so far away from it yourself, even if you are now on the path to making it happen (and it *will* happen if you truly change your mindset!). When I first started working out, for example, I remember that, even though I was ready to embark on the journey to change my lifestyle, I still found myself constantly talking myself out of it. A little voice inside my head would start negotiating with me, saying, 'You don't need to go to the gym tonight, you've had a really stressful day.' That little voice can be a right fucker: it gets into your head, starts negotiating with you and before you know it, it's won.

That voice can be incredibly persuasive because, guess what? It knows everything about you: every little nook and cranny it can get into to prise the whole thing wide open. It will use your own thoughts against you, and have you turn back to your old, comfort-zone way of living. The voice is not that evil, really. It wants to keep you safe, protected and comfortable, after all. But when you want growth, it's not who you need on your side.

Alongside the little negotiating voice, I also had this resounding worry that I was somehow 'losing' myself. Losing what had made me 'me': my quirks and resistances. I wasn't an 'exercise person'; those people were all annoying show-offs. I wasn't like that! I'd never been like that. I didn't *want* to be like that. So, every step of progress also felt like I was shedding my old skin, and some of that felt sad. I felt like I wasn't going to be fun and quirky and witty and sarcastic anymore. I would be a healthy, fit, BORE. But you know what? That didn't happen. I'm still me, but much healthier, more energised and in the best shape of my life.

This negotiating voice can really hinder or even halt your progress. The voice and the 'old you' team up, and together they can overpower the part of you that wants to move forward and take the positive route. They will try to pin you down and make you chicken out.

Let me just say: all of these feelings are *normal*.

If this has been happening to you while you've been reading this book and trying to make changes, or you come to feel this way later, after you put this book down and start working on your journey, it's OK. You're not a loser. It doesn't mean you can't change. Do you know how long it took me to become an 'exercise person'?

Two years. Two years of non-stop back and forth. And that's just the time when I had a personal trainer who was constantly holding me accountable and trying to motivate me. I'm not even counting the years before that, all the time it had taken me mentally to get to a place where I would even consider going into a gym.

Mindset changes can be hard work. They require consistency, effort, willpower and, most importantly, the ability to ignore your negotiator and your old self: the 'enemies of change'.

Because I know what a big shift this is, I want to take you through some coping mechanisms that may help you find the journey a little less choppy.

WHEN YOUR FRIENDS DON'T GET IT

Growing up, it's likely you formed friendships with people who had similar interests to you. As you get older, sometimes your lifestyle choices or family set-up can be what provides an environment for connection: for example, a couple with children are likely to have a lot of other friends who also have kids. Of course we don't only have friends who look, sound and behave exactly like us, but we often have some shared common ground. A lot of our similarities can be around mindset and, as I have increasingly noticed, financial situation.

You may find that your friendship circles are largely formed of people who are in and around the same financial bracket as you. Often, we form friendship circles with people who think and act in the same way as us because we have shared viewpoints of the world and it's comfortable. While the fact that what you all earn is similar doesn't provide much to worry about, the money mindset of the group does. Do your friends share your old negative mindset around money?

On your journey to having a positive money mindset, you will find that your language changes and the choices you make will be different. It's likely you will want to start changing other things, like the places you go to hang out, or where you shop. It's all part of the evolution of your mindset. You will start to want better for yourself and, naturally, that will change how you do things. You are upgrading your internal hardwiring. While you are in this transition phase, certain friendships may become a little hard to navigate.

When people see a friend make sudden, drastic changes, especially a friend who previously had a similar mindset or lifestyle to them, it can be challenging. The steps you take to improve your life can inadvertently cause some people to realise that they, too, have been stuck in a negative mindset or their own 'comfort zone'. Instead of finding the fact that you are trying to progress motivational or inspiring, however, they may find it difficult. It might make them feel as if they are not good enough. This can cause them to start getting defensive of their current lifestyle, or even go as far as to criticise you for trying to make changes.

As you learned in the opening chapters of this book, money is a very emotional subject with deeply entrenched roots, so it can cause all kinds of emotional reactions, and they often don't make sense. Your friend may not even realise this is what they are doing. They might say things like, 'I'm just trying to save you from being disappointed.' They're not: they are the ones who are disappointed. They're disappointed that you have made a positive change before they had the strength to do so themselves.

It doesn't come from a nasty place. It comes from a vulnerable place.

That is why I will not tell you to 'cut them out' as some people might. I don't believe in that. Some 'friends' might be worth removing, for sure: you'll know that's the case if their behaviour turns from a projection of their own fears into nastiness. If this happens, it may be worth taking a break until your friend is in a better place to cope with your changes. However, most people simply do not realise what is happening or why they are reacting as they are. As you've probably seen, we can be so out of sync with our deepest desires and wants that all this crap gets on top of them – and we believe the crap. So no, I don't advise you to cut friends out completely. Instead, I suggest you look at limiting your conversations about money when you're around them, until you are much further down the line with your journey and can't be so easily swayed.

In the early stages, it can be extremely easy to be pulled back into your old mindset by your own thoughts, let alone when a third party starts getting involved, too. Your friends can add to the internal voices of doubt, making you think you will never be able to change, or that you're not good enough to, even if they don't use such harsh words.

HERE ARE A FEW TIPS IN DEALING WITH FRIENDS WHO MAY NOT BE AS EXCITED ABOUT YOUR MONEY JOURNEY AS YOU ARE:

- Don't tell them straight away. Work on your mindset until you feel that you can control your own inner thoughts first. Then, and only then, might you be able to cope with an external voice entering the mix.

- Keep the conversation focused around other things. You have many shared interests, and many of those will be influenced by money, sure, but they aren't all directly about money. Stick to other activities and conversations that won't open you up to criticism.
- It's perfectly OK to have some friends for certain things and others for money talk.
- Don't fall into the same negative language around money as before, even if they do.
- Change the conversation! If things do start going in a direction that you feel may be pulling you into negative money stuff, don't go there. Change the subject.

I know some of these tips may seem harsh. After all, these are your friends, and they may often confide in you about their own money struggles. I know it's hard, but while you're in the transition phase of sorting yourself out, you can't always be there for everyone else. You have to fit your own oxygen mask before you can help others, you know? You won't be able to progress with your positive money mindset if those around you keep trying to pull you back into negative money conversations. All it will do is provide more evidence to the parts of your brain that don't want to believe change is possible – the enemies of progress.

Once you feel that you have moved forward enough, you can, of course, go back to having conversations where you provide support and love for your friends who are struggling financially. I do it often now, but only because I know that:

a) I can be a positive support and influence about money rather than just pushing them further into victim mode;

and

b) it will bounce off me. It doesn't make me question my new money beliefs or make me start thinking negatively about money again.

I make sure to take these conversations on a more positive journey, by guiding my friends towards something that might help, like the things that helped me in the early stages.

Your friends might not be ready to undertake the journey you have taken. That's OK. Just think about how long it took you to get here. And because we're all different, and some of us face different disadvantages, it will take some longer than others.

Remember to try and be a positive influence for your friends. It may be hard for them to adjust at first but, trust me, it will pay off in the long run. The most exciting thing you can probably imagine is if you and your closest friends could all shift to a positive money mindset. Imagine the power of a whole group of friends all speaking, acting and responding to money situations with positivity and joy! I can tell you from first-hand experience that, after a few years, this is exactly what has happened with my own circle of friends. I've really never experienced anything like it. I've watched my friends go from strength to strength in their businesses, wealth, health, relationships and more. Not only that, but we are all so positive and supportive of each other and where we are going. I genuinely think that this support has led to increased successes for all of us.

WHEN YOUR PARTNER DOESN'T GET IT

One of the most frequent concerns I hear from the students of the online Money and Manifesting course I run with Jen, is that they don't feel supported by their partner when starting to focus on their money mindset and manifestation. The words 'hippy' and 'woo-woo' come up a lot – and honestly, I get it! I can totally see why it would seem that way from the outside, especially when we're talking about things that aren't tangible, like thought patterns or 'the universe'.

The resistance we can often feel from our friends is, I think, even more amplified with our partners. It can feel like we're either in things together or having a power struggle. Often the partners who seem to be being unsupportive are dealing with feelings of concern and worry that their partner is being 'ripped off' or getting their hopes up about something that will end up letting them down. But I think this process can also show us how our partner REALLY feels about money, and perhaps reveal something about their own money programming.

Sometimes these revelations can be sad, worrying or even distressing. Some people have, really and truly, experienced some unfair shit in their life. And, as we know from doing our work around programming, if left unaddressed, these things can really affect the way we live our day-to-day lives. As I've said before, money is a super-emotional subject for many people, and just because you're on the journey to a happy and rich life doesn't mean your partner will be on board. This might surprise or disappoint you. You'd totally think they would get it, right? After all, if your partner loves and cares for you, why wouldn't they support you? Especially as your soon-to-be abundant lifestyle will probably have a very direct effect on them; so, why wouldn't they be all for it?

It's complicated.

Again, your progress may trigger difficult feelings for them. Be prepared to encounter these, just as in your friendship circles. The difference here, though, is that you can't just spend less time with your partner, or only have conversations with them about certain things. This is someone you've chosen to spend your life with, after all.

So, how can you deal with it?

If your partner is someone who doesn't really believe in any kind of spiritual stuff, it's probably best to talk about the more practical sides of being positive about money, instead of the magical. Hold off on the 'universe' talk and instead communicate what you are experiencing using the kind of words that they would use themselves. For example, I know the word 'manifest' can sound really hippy-ish to a lot of people, and the Law of Attraction can have a lot of airy-fairy connotations. But talking about being open to opportunities or having a positive attitude doesn't seem to bother people as much. Sometimes it's best to just talk about how you are working on your money mindset.

Remember also that your partner is likely to want to protect you from anything they might think is a bit dodgy, or a situation where you might be taken advantage of. Your partner might worry that you are being sucked in by a new fad or be scared that you might get excited and piss away your life savings (at worst) or, at best, be left with hurt feelings. We don't want the ones we love to experience disappointment on any level.

Assure your partner that you're not going to do anything crazy! First, you're a grown-up and can handle your own expectations. Secondly, you could literally work through everything in this book without spending a penny (apart from buying the book in the first place). It's more about mindset than spending.

Sometimes when you are on a new path of positivity, it can highlight areas where your partner is being negative.

It's easy to start critiquing or pointing things out, but don't criticise or shame any of their negative money behaviour. Even if you notice it, they might not yet. If you start pointing it out, they will feel attacked, which is never the start to a productive conversation.

I like to open up the conversation by asking someone how they were brought up around money. What feelings did they experience as a child about it? What phrases did they hear? How did their parents interact with money? Even if you do nothing else, having this conversation with your partner will help you to figure out the map of the world they have when it comes to money. It will help you to understand how they think. Many people from our Money and Manifesting course have come back to me and said that the course pushed them to start conversations about money with their partner that they would otherwise never have had, and that it has brought them closer together as a result.

Ask your partner for their support. Regardless of whether your partner agrees with what you're doing, you can ask them to support you instead of criticising. Be honest about your feelings. Say what is true for you – perhaps you are fed up with being broke and want to make a better life for both of you; or maybe you're excited about having your own financial freedom so you don't need to lean on them so much, thus taking the pressure off them. Whatever is true for you, share it and ask for their support with whatever it might take for you to move forward.

Let the changes in your life speak for themselves. We

often get excited about new things we are trying but, just as with your friends, at first it can be a challenging time, and you might feel quite vulnerable. People will share their opinions and that can be influential, even if they don't mean it to be. So, let the positive money changes you start to experience do all the talking. Most of the time, once a partner has seen how much of a difference changing your money mindset makes – and for some people it is literally life changing – they come on board. Nothing will make this experience more enjoyable and productive for you than if your partner gets on board, because then you can start putting your dream life into practice together. It can be such an exciting time when a couple open up to each other about their honest feelings about money and make plans for their future together.

This doesn't happen for everyone, though, and sometimes getting your partner on board (or even getting them to accept the journey you're on) can take a long time. Be patient. Think about it: if it was the other way around, it might take you a while to get your head around it, too. Often, once you start seeing real results, other people will come around.

For example, my husband has always been supportive of whatever I want to do and how I want to think, but he wasn't really down with the whole 'manifesting' thing at first. He probably deemed any positive results to be pure coincidence. And I couldn't even get him started on something like crystals or tarot reading! He wasn't rude about it: I think he found it a little bit amusing. When I started working on my money mindset, I shared what I was doing in my sessions, the questions I was asked and what my responses were. Jason and I would have quite long and in-depth conversations about how we grew up around money. But he wasn't really buying into the 'I wrote this down and then it happened' part. But after these weird synchronicities kept happening, he started to take notice.

WHEN YOUR FAMILY DON'T GET IT

As with your partner, you can't just 'drop' family members, yet sometimes, I've heard, they can be the most unforgiving when it comes to talking about money. I'm not gonna lie: this is really tough.

When it comes to family members not being able to vibe with your new mindset, try and channel as much empathy as possible. Think back to what we learned at the start of the book about conditioning and programming. For example, how were your parents or grandparents brought up around money? If they had a particularly hard childhood, they really may not want to discuss it. They might also be worrying about the journey you are embarking on and feeling anxious that you might end up feeling let down.

Even though these people are your family and may have raised you, it doesn't stop them from projecting their own fears and insecurities on to you. Try not to take it personally. This goes for anyone sending judgement your way. When people are mean, or put you down, or try to sway you from something you're excited about, they could actually be looking out for you, in a weird way. Behaviour like this can come from a good place, as nasty as it might seem. It might also come from a hurt place, in which case you showing empathy for their situation will go a long way. I know it takes a lot to be able to rise above the feelings of frustration when you just want their support, but it goes so much further than that. As much as we love our friends, family and partners, sometimes it's really hard for them to deal with their own internal issues, so you may see that they struggle with this.

HOW HAVE OTHERS WORKED THROUGH IT?

Every situation is different, and you may find that you have an easy time with the people around you, which would be great! You might even find that they start asking you questions about how they can go on a similar journey after they see the new, positive relationship you have with money.

In case this doesn't happen, though, I thought you may find it useful to hear how some of my past Money and Manifesting course students had coped with various friends, family members or partners not really supporting their money journey.

I asked my past students to share their advice with you, and here's what they said:

I found myself really annoyed with friends that showed resistance at first, and disappointed in them, because I'd expected them to be supportive of me growing into something new and exciting. I really do believe in good energy when you are trying to manifest, so I avoided speaking about it to people that I thought would be 'Negative Nancies' at the time, as I didn't want it to dull my vibe.

I'd tell them when things were almost finalised or nearly done, so their inability to get on board wasn't affecting how I felt or my ability to manifest and be happy.

Over time, as I got more confident with it and the stakes didn't feel as high, I spoke to some of them, drawing them into the journey slowly. They didn't need to believe in it or do it themselves, but I felt taking them along on the journey, bit by bit, helped them get on board, and allowed me to have a relationship with them, while still maintaining my sanity and focus on growth.

SMITA

I talk to people a lot about the Money and Manifesting course. Mainly people think I'm mad and that I'm going to come down to earth with a big bump, but they do seem to like the fact that I've taken a 'risk'. Since the course, my main takeaway is to charge what excites you and don't be desperate for work: it'll come, and it has. My parents are super-supportive but also super-cautious, so are scared I'll fail at self-employment.

This year, in six months, I will have earned a few grand shy of what I earned throughout the whole of last year, so while people think I'm woo-woo, the power of the mind works. As long as I believe in me . . . I think I'll be all right.

AMY

I've cut a few friends out as I realised that they were carrying a lot of negative energy and I felt drained whenever I saw them. I didn't like who I was when I was around them. Since doing this, I have flourished in confidence and attracted better people into my life. A few of my other friends have started to get on board, which I love to see. They thought I was a bit weird at first but they commented how much more positive they feel after seeing me, so ya know, just spreading the love!

As for family, that's a whole different ball game. They have so much deep-rooted stuff about money. I can see clearly now why I was like I was, and I've still got a lot to shift. If they talk negatively about money, I try to take a step back from the conversation and try to slowly drip-feed positive vibes. Sometimes it can work, sometimes it doesn't.

BRIDIE

I definitely feel that I have unconsciously pulled away from people who have a more negative mindset and I now spend way more time with those who have a positive mindset in all regards. It wasn't intentional, but

I've noticed it happen. When I am in a position where I'm mixing with those with a negative mindset, I will always reframe their thinking and do it with a smile on my face, but I find it a drag sometimes and an energy zap, so keeping those interactions to a minimum is a priority for me.

Protecting my own energy and my family's energy is super-important. My mum told me that my five-year-old told her off the other day when she complained about the bad weather. He said, 'Rain is good because we need it for the plants to grow!' I think she really took that on board, being told by a kid! So, I guess not cutting people out completely is also important because we can teach others how to make these positive shifts, too.

REBECCA

While my husband has used my change in language when it comes to purposefully talking about money positively as an opportunity to take the piss out of me, as it all seems to him to be a bit woo-woo, in reality he actively encourages me (in his own piss-taking way). It is slowly contributing to how he now talks about money and the abundance which is coming his way.

RONKE

I think it is such a hard concept for so many people to get their heads around that when I encountered resistance, it didn't surprise me. What I did was, rather than try to explain the concept, I just used examples and pointed out the positive. I quit my very well-paid job to start my biz and everyone was so worried about me not having enough money – blah, blah, the usual. So, I refused to talk about money. Instead, I let them see how my mental health was improving, how I was less stressed, how I was so bloody happy! Then people began to catch on. Positivity is infectious. Now they can see I might earn a fraction of what I did (for now) but my lifestyle has only improved.

NAT

I recognise that my other half isn't into spiritual stuff, but that doesn't mean I don't talk about it from time to time. I knew he was taking at least some of it on board when he listened to a podcast about a fighter raising his vibration before a fight! So, the key is, it needs to be in their own time AND in their language.

VICTORIA

No matter who is or isn't down with your new outlook, remember that it is not personal. If you try to have a conversation or positive money experience with someone and they don't want to go there, just make a mental note not to do it again with that person. You will soon start attracting people to you who are in a similar headspace and want to have those open conversations around money and hold each other to account in terms of keeping high-vibe.

We have a private Facebook group for our students and I take so much delight in seeing them come and share amazing and exciting things that have happened to them. Some say that it's the only place they feel safe and comfortable sharing the good things that have happened to them, because they know the other members of the group won't see it as bragging or showing off. It's so supportive: there are endless amounts of congratulations and the group shows genuine joy and excitement for people's good fortune. Imagine if you could have a group of people around you like that, where you didn't have to check yourself before going all in and openly sharing your pride, excitement and joy when something amazing happens to you. How much faster would you be able to shift your mindset? As a society, we have been conditioned to downplay our wins – you know, the whole 'this old thing' talk. We worry about coming off as someone who is boasting, because we know it will be taken as purposefully trying to make someone else feel crap about their situation. It's really sad that we've reached this stage, never able to celebrate our good fortune for fear of how others may feel.

Remember, how others feel because of their own personal situation is not something you can control. Don't hold yourself back from enjoying the great things that come your way because you are worried about how someone else may react.

Their reaction is not your business.

What *is* your business is keeping your vibe high and your mind positive.

$ *EXERCISE* $

Make a list of anyone in your life who you see as having a positive mindset around money, and who could be your cheerleader going forward. Open up a conversation with them about how they feel about money.

_____

_____

_____

_____

_____

_____

_____

_____

€

CONCLUSION

THE MONEY IS COMING!

When I told people that I was writing a book about money, a lot of them thought it would be a guide to savings accounts, interest rates or negotiating a pay rise. You know the drill: 'Don't buy that latte, save that money and, in twenty years, you might have enough for a house deposit.' Not I'm not shitting on that sort of stuff: for some, it works.

But I wanted to focus on you making MORE, not spending LESS.

Personally, I find the idea of budgeting, cutting out fun and making sacrifices very low-vibe. And if you haven't realised by now, our whole focus is to stay HIGH-VIBE!

This goes against everything we are taught. We are taught we shouldn't have fun. That it's indulgent to spend on things we love. To cut back, stay in, look for the cheapest option. To negotiate on every deal, to work our money the hardest and squeeze it the tightest.

But what if that just left us feeling low?

I want you to walk away from reading this book and realise that, by doing whatever you can to stay in a happy, positive mindset that feels GOOD about money, you will attract more.

Go where feels good and intuitively right to you. You know more than you think. The media and social narrative about money (especially around women) is that we don't know what's best for ourselves. We are silly girls who spend too much on shoes and make-up. We are scared and panicked into 'being sensible' and 'saving for a rainy day', but what if we don't expect the worst to happen? What if we expect the very best to happen, and believe that it can happen for us?

It's not a case of being frivolous, wasting money or spending what we don't have.

It's about avoiding things that make us feel really down about money. It's about looking for the silver lining, even in the crappiest of circumstances; it's about having a strong mindset, believing in ourselves and, most of all, having the will to believe that anything is possible.

It will give you hope.

And hope is incredibly important.

Because hope leads to excitement, and I've seen excitement to be a very, very potent emotion when manifesting more money. It's like money-attraction steroids.

Whatever you can do to step into that excitement – which is safe and feels intuitively good for you, deep down – do it.

The subject of money-making seems so practical and tangible, but the reality that I've experienced is that it is the emotion and mindset behind it that truly make the difference to how much money you can have in your life.

If I haven't shouted it loud enough yet, here I go for one last time.

To make money, you first have to become the kind of person who can make money.

The person who believes in themselves and knows their worth. Who believes that things will work out, and that there is a positive lesson to be taken from everything. That person knows they are destined for greatness, no matter what their current financial situation is.

'Rich' is a mindset.

And if you're reading this and you're still not sure you can become that person, I'm here to tell you that you can. YOU BLOODY WELL CAN. I've experienced it myself, and countless students of our Money and Manifesting course have, too. It will work for you, if you just suspend your doubts and disbelief for a second and step into what could be out there for you.

Allow yourself to open up to the possibilities of money just showing up for you in weird, wonderful ways. You don't know what could happen, and neither do I. We like to think we can control every money move. But what if money had its own energy, its own flow, and it moved to where it felt a high vibration?

I want to leave you with an important mantra. It's a mantra that has got me through the toughest of times, the most angst-ridden, low moments. It's a mantra that has been the antidote to those tough times, every time.

This mantra will give you hope and optimism. It EXPECTS the very best to happen.

Please take this forward on your journey.

Whisper it to yourself, even when it feels like it makes no sense, and shout it out loud in big, bold excitement when money starts arriving for you out of nowhere.

That mantra?

THE MONEY IS COMING.

WHAT'S NEXT?

You can find all of the accompanying audio and PDF worksheets mentioned throughout this book at www. themoneyiscoming.com.

If you've enjoyed having a taste and would like to continue your journey of attracting more money into your life, come and take a look at the Money and Manifesting course I run with Jen. It's a thirty-day intensive programme that will change how you think about money for the better, forever. Think about everything you have learned here and imagine that on crack. You'll be surrounded by a group of like-minded individuals who will lift you up, celebrate your wins with you and keep you feeling high-vibe.

You can learn more about the course, take our free money personality quiz and register your interest at www. nobullbusinessschool.com/mmschool.

I would love to hear your stories and experiences. Please share them with me online by tagging me @sarahakwisombe, and use the hashtag #themoneyiscoming

REFERENCES

1. 'Social conditioning', Wikipedia. https://en.wikipedia.org/wiki/Social_conditioning
2. Rogers, Carl R., 1959. 'A theory of therapy, personality, and interpersonal relationships, as developed in the client-centered framework.' https://pdfs.semanticscholar.org/cd4f/6ead952372d350ff792d212cb9d6de9c5f48.pdfVery
3. Alberti, Robert E. and Emmons, Michael L., 1970. *Your Perfect Right: A Guide to Assertive Behavior*, Loose Leaf *197*.
4. 'Neuroplasticity', Wikipedia. https://en.wikipedia.org/wiki/Neuroplasticity
5. Aravena, P, et al. 2012. 'Grip Force Reveals the Context Sensitivity of Language-Induced Motor Activity during "Action Words" Processing: Evidence from Sentential Negation.' https://journals.plos.org/plosone/article?id=10.1371/journal.pone.0050287
6. Definition of coincidence. https://www.lexico.com/definition/coincidence
7. 'Synchronicity', Wikipedia. https://en.wikipedia.org/wiki/Synchronicity
8. Ekeocha, Tracy C. 2015. 'The effects of visualization & guided imagery in sports performance.' https://digital.library.txstate.edu/bitstream/handle/10877/5548/EKEOCHA-THESIS-2015.pdf?sequence=1

ACKNOWLEDGEMENTS

Jen MacFarlane! Where would I be now if I hadn't met you? It seems weird to think that we've never met in person yet have such a strong bond and have changed so many lives together. You are a special person and I hope that this book gives us a reason to finally be in the same room. You know that Money and Manifesting retreat has to happen, right?! I couldn't have written this without you. You have taught me so much and truly changed my life and mindset for the better. I hope you get to be rich beyond your wildest dreams, because you deserve it.

To my mum and dad: Mum, who read over chapters with me to make sure they actually made sense, and who helped me understand the psychological theories in layman's terms. Thank you for answering every text and listening to me when I was stressed out about getting the book done on time. Dad, thank you for giving me the confidence to be outspoken and stand up for what I believe in, because without that I wouldn't be in the position I am. To both of you, for passing on your money beliefs, even if I had to rejig a couple of them. When I am rich, I will take us all on holiday, and you'll be thankful for that rejigging.

To anyone who has ever taken our Money and Manifesting course: you guys are amazing. The way you show up and support each other makes me feel all fuzzy inside every time we run the course. Seeing your transformations and watching you give each other advice and lift each other up has truly been a blessing and I hope this book means that more people get to experience life inside our brilliant little community. Being part of your conversations gave me so many thinking points to explore in this book, so I really want to thank you for that.

To Annie and Will: you guys didn't have much involvement with this, but you always keep my feet on the ground and my ego completely and utterly deflated in the best possible way. Love you losers.

To Lois, Sophie, Jemma, Milly and Bex: I never thought I'd have a group of girl mates like you. You all consistently kept me feeling good throughout the process of writing this book and I know you will all be championing it when it comes out. Well, you better.

To darling Marley: thank you for sneaking into my office and drawing pictures to keep me entertained. Thanks for the whiteboard chart we made, which we filled out to show how many words I'd done. You drew smiley faces and wrote 'Keep going, nearly there!' You don't know how much I needed that sometimes.

To Jillian and the team at Piatkus, and Jane and co. at

Graham Maw Christie: thank you for believing in me enough to put this out.

And to Jason – darling, darling Jason. Honestly, I don't know how I could do any of this without you behind me. It literally wouldn't happen. You are what makes me great and I owe you so, so much. Now let's have a holiday to celebrate?!

INDEX